DEAR
GIRL CHILD

Letter to the girls, ladies, women loved by the Lord

CAROL NKAMBULE

ISBN : 978-0-620-69139-0

eISBN : 978-0-620-69142-0

Published by Author using Kingdom Anchored publishing services, P O Box 3794, Nelspruit, 1200.

Contributions by Nomsa Mashele - Chapter 13

Edited by Morongwe Raphasha

Cover designed by Bathabile Makutu

Website: www.carolnkambule.co.za

www.kingdomanchored.co.za

Email – carolnkambule@gmail.com

Contents

Dedication

To all the girls out there, Daddy's beloved and precious ones. You who are wonderfully and fearfully made. The last ones to be created, God's master piece. This is for you, with love from our Father.

This is for us girls, young and old.

A long, love letter to you.

Jesus loves you

Introduction

Dear Girl Child, the beloved of the Lord, the one made in the image of your Father in heaven, this letter is for you. With this very long letter, the Lord seeks to set the record straight, in your heart, mind and spirit. This is the heart of God reconciling you to Himself. Receive the words with gladness, knowing that Your Father in heaven is mindful of you.

Many words have been spoken, God has been misrepresented in your hearing. Let this letter correct these misstatements. Let the wrong words be erased out of your mind. Let your spirit arise and be aligned with the Spirit of God, your mind be renewed so that you will move to the fullness of the will of God for your life.

You are not a mistake, irrespective of how you came into the world. You are not a second class citizen. You are not a tool to be used and discarded. Remember, God did not take you directly out of dust. He had to make the first human being, and in perfecting His first created being, He used that one to create an even beautifully crafted and delicate being. You are not second thought, but you are a perfect fit.

Let the words in this long letter correct your misgivings, your misunderstanding, and your wrong perception so that you will rise to enjoy the life God has planned for you. As God said, *"Owe no one anything except to love one another."* Romans 13:8. That is the part you will play on this earth, in all that you do to others, let it be out of love. The Lord has loved you from the beginning of time.

You are a Girl Child, in whatever stage of life you are, you are a child of God. You may be in your early teens, you may be in your teens, in your youth, you may also be an adult or even an old woman, and you are still a Girl Child to your

Father in heaven.

Hear these words, let them shape and sharpen you, let them change you and build you up. As God said to Joshua, let the word of God not depart from your mouth, meditate on it day and night. You are God's masterpiece!

1

It all starts with God

Dear Girl Child, remember where it all started. When God created all things on this earth, and the earth was ready to be inhabited by beings, that are human and are like God, He made man. After all these things, and man was on this earth, there was still a void in the life of man. Remember how God searched to and fro in the earth, there was no companion suitable for man. As God had made man out of the dust of the earth and breathed into his nostrils and he became a living being, you would have thought He would do the same when forming a companion for this man, but it was not so.

You see, man was formed on this earth and God saw that His workmanship was good, but, in making a companion for man, God decided to change His technique. God went to the man He created and made him to sleep. He did not want to be disturbed for He was making someone special and delicate. God went into the rib, the part that keeps the heart and all delicate parts in a human safe and protected, there He found a piece He used to form a companion for a man. You were created, and you came alive Girl Child. You belonged to God, just as man did. You were released to earth together with man and blessed together with man, but you were formed differently. You were made out of a living being that was just sleeping.

The first Girl Child, called a woman, named Eve, was presented to man and he was pleased.

He had found a companion and loved her. He took her as his own and lived in the garden with her. He had confidence in her to the point of accepting the fruit which was forbidden, he ate the fruit. Then man began to see her as the woman God gave to him. Man blamed her for all his troubles with the Lord.

Yes, she had taken of the fruit and ate, she had sinned against the Lord, but God put this sin on man.

Here is the beauty of the Lord concerning you Girl Child. Even though she was wrong, God chose to redeem human kind by the very same species that caused the trouble in the first place. God could have chosen that the seed of man would crush the head of the serpent, the deceiver, but He chose you.

How gracious is our Father in heaven? In His innumerable mercies and endless grace, He still chose a woman.

You are not a second rate citizen. You are blessed to the core, to the very place that brings out human kind. Over the years God has entrusted you to carry humanity in your belly. No matter how powerful a man can be, only the Girl Child will grow to carry even the male child and bring children to this earth. You are entrusted with the multiplication with which God blessed both males and females.

Therefore, Girl Child, look around you, every human being on this earth was carried by a woman. That is how special you are. Our Redeemer, the Lord Jesus, was carried by your kind for the number of months required for a baby to grow in the womb, she gave birth at the appointed time.

You may be blamed for some of the wrong things that happens on this earth, but God chose you. You may be hurt and be blamed for it, but God still trusts you to carry life through.

You may be seen as the one who came second, but you were the perfection of the human creation. You may have been taken out of man, but you were with man when man was blessed. So take heart daughter of God, you are loved by your Father in heaven.

Knowing your position in God is as crucial as life itself, for if you do not know it, you will be tossed to and fro by the wind. Some will tell you that your sins are too many, God will not forgive you. Remember the woman caught in adultery, she was brought to Jesus for judgement. Where was the man, for no one can commit adultery alone?

Jesus showed them a better way. He showed them that none of them had no sin and all have sinned and fell short of the glory of God, but Jesus had come, glory to God. He came to save humanity and He came through a woman. Remember how His own mother was almost abandoned by Joseph because she had conceived a child before they were married? Jesus knew how a woman could be rejected by society, as if there were better species.

You, Girl Child, are chosen by God. Let this redemption that came through the womb of a woman not pass you by. Do not let circumstances and your own deeds prohibit you from recognizing that redemption has come to you. Jesus became the Lord of His own mother. Who are you to think you cannot be redeemed? His mother was a virgin before she conceived, but she was not a saint. She was of the seed of fallen man and also needed redemption, she carried redemption into this earth, yet she also needed to be redeemed.

The only thing expected and required of you is to take Jesus into your life. Let it all begin with Jesus. It does not matter how far you have gone in life. It does not matter how bad you think your sins are. It does not matter how embarrassed and shameful you feel.

Just take your place right next to the woman caught in adultery, imagine yourself holding her hand and receiving forgiveness for your own sins. Jesus did not condemn her, even though her sin was great. I ask myself what happened to that man she was caught with. He did not come to receive forgiveness from Jesus. Imagine in the last day, when the dead rise, that man facing the punishment for the sin he committed with a woman whose sins have been forgiven.

You may have accepted Jesus in your life, but you turned back and denied Him like Peter did when trouble came. You may have committed sins because of the trouble you faced in life, but here is Jesus, He is within breath, He waits for your call. He has sorted out the accusers, He has reminded them of their own sins and the punishment that follows. You on the other hand, have a chance with Jesus, go for the King of kings.

Let it all start and end with God. He loves you regardless of what you have done or where you have been. Remember Hannah in the bible? She had no child because God had closed up her womb. She looked for a child from her husband and found none. She looked for a child in her own tears, but found none. She came to the realization that there is only one who gives life and there was a place she could communicate with Him and put her case before Him. She went to seek the face of God in the tabernacle. Her son was not with her husband but was with God. She had to go on her knees to get her son.

Hannah cried to the Lord to the point of being seen as a drunk woman. She poured her heart out to the Lord. It was God who knew where her child was. God granted her request and she conceived a child, she named him Samuel. You see, Girl Child, your things will not be released from heaven until, and unless you go to He who inhabits the heavens, who sits enthroned in His holy habitation. It is on your knees Girl Child that your things will be released. They are with God.

Your life is with God,

Your children are with God,

Your husband is with God,

Your provision is with God,

Your safety is in God,

Your forgiveness is in God,

Your love is tucked up in the heart of God,

Everything starts and ends with God.

If I were to look back at my own life, I was lost but I am found, I was weak but now I am strong, I was sad but now my joy is in the Lord. My sins were way too many, if I were to count them I would have to dig a hole and hide there first.

If anyone were to come now and point a finger at me concerning what I did in the past, I will point them to the direction of the cross. I have no business in my past. It does not matter how big you think my sins were, God has forgiven me all of them.

I started to truly live when I found Jesus, I mean to say, when Jesus found me. I found meaning to life, I found my purpose. I found direction for my life. My purpose was not in my job, for if it were, I would not have written my first book.

If I look back at the life I left behind, I realize that I miss nothing. I do not miss the company and destructive actions. In fact, a lot of the people I knew then have died. I found life in Jesus, it is by His grace not by my works. All I needed was to answer His call.

I was raised up a Jehovah's Witness, and read the bible and still did not know God. I could tell you what the different books said, but not what the voice of God said concerning my life. I was found by Jesus in 2009. I found out that I had not scratched even the surface of the word of God. I found that I had not started living a fulfilled life, where nothing else matters but God. When He matters in your life, He brings all that should matter in your life to you.

Would you take Him, would you stretch out your hand to God and trust Him with your life and your sustenance? Would you depend on Him even when it does not seem that your answer is coming anytime soon?

God awaits in anticipation, be reconciled with your maker. The Bible says, angels rejoice in heaven when one sinner comes to Christ. They rejoice when they see a reconciliation with the Father. The enemy wants you in his corner so he can destroy you.

There is neither joy nor peace without God. Money will not make you happy as you will continue chasing it. Men will not make you happy as they come with burdens and may end up hurting you.

There is so much to be done and experienced, with God in your life, success is certain.

2

You are loved

Beloved child of God, let these words enter and find rest in your heart. Let this reminder never depart from your mind. Let your spirit take this truth and keep it to everlasting. You are loved by God!

You have looked for love in the wrong places, from the wrong people. You have elevated tangible things to a position of the definition of love. You have put other human beings in the place which must be occupied by God first, so His love can fill that place and love will overflow to others, and you will receive love back. You have trusted people with your love and forgot that only God can be trusted and He is worthy of your trust.

You have been disappointed in your kind of love. You have defined love wrongly and it has come short. You have not gotten what you have desired. You still look in the wrong places for love. You think that the validation of man equates to love. You think the company of your friends defines what love is. You think money is the same a love. You think that the touch of man is love.

Let the Lord define for you what love is, daughter of the Most High God:

"Love suffers long and is kind; love does not envy; love does not parade itself; is not puffed up; does not behave rudely, does not seek its own, is not provoked, thinks no evil; does not rejoice in iniquity, but rejoices in the truth; bears all things, believes all

things, hopes all things, endures all things. Love never fails." 1 Corinthians 13:4-8.

Girl, by now you realize that what you thought was love does not match up with the definition of love according to the word of God.

It may feel good when you get your pair of shoes, but they come at a price. It may feel good when you get many likes on social networks, but that is not love. You may feel good being the center of attention, but those people want something from you. You will realize that it is not love when things change, people leave, then you are alone.

There is one that loves you regardless of your situation. There is one that loves you and shows you by acts of kindness, of patience, of humility. There is love that does not require anything back from you, that is unconditional love. You see Girl Child, as you grow older and wiser, your body may end up different, and your figure may fade away for a while and love does not change but remains with you.

It is in your failures that you will realize who actually has true love for you. It is in your weakness and bad times that you will remain with love. For the word says love suffers long. When you are frustrated and take it out on those around you, love will remain and help pick you up.

However, the one who is patient with you, is love. When you fail, love is there all the time. Love reminds you that you can do better. Love does not say, since you are no longer wealthy, you are not worth the trouble. Love does not say, since you are frustrated because your life is not as you expected it to be, you are not good enough. Imagine if God was impatient with you, where will you be? Think back, how many times you have failed to do what God asked of you. A simple instruction from the Lord seemed too much for you.

I have been there many times, even on this day that I write this letter to you.

You see, the Lord woke me up this morning, 4th August 2015, very early in the morning and gave me this letter to write. I am not a morning person as they say, and for some reason the Lord has deemed it fit to give me messages in the early hours of the morning. Couple this with the fact that it was windy and very cold, I took my hand out from under the blanket and quickly put it back. I felt the wind on the one side of my body right under the blanket.

I knew this was a call to wake up and write, but it was too cold, but Daddy, in His patience still talked to me in my half co-operation with Him. He took me through all the chapters of this long letter. I put them on the note pad on my cellphone. He took me through the words in each chapter, the main points, but then I went back to sleep. I had a bad dream, and I woke up and prayed. I asked for forgiveness. God did not send me the bad dream, but my conscience and the enemy dealt with me.

When I finished praying, I took the laptop and began to worship. Then I earnestly asked the Lord to forgive me for ignoring His instructions in the morning. I asked for the Spirit of the Lord to come and fill me again with the message. I asked for guidance and I asked for the rain. I put on music and the Lord told me to start writing, typing so to say. This was the beginning, I was at home with eye problems and in between wiping my eyes I was typing this message.

What would I do if God was impatient with me? Where would the message be? How many times have I not listened to His instructions and He still gave me a second, third, fourth and countless chances. It is because God is love and therefore He is patient.

As for you child of God, can you honestly say you are patient? Can you see that every time you and I become impatient with others, we are actually acting outside of love? Lord help me! Rejoice daughter of the Most High God, for your Father in heaven is patient with you and He is love.

Now that you know the patience part of the love of God, would you begin to disassociate yourself with all that is impatient in you? Some other people are not able to do the things you are able to do, be patient with them. If your parents fail in any area of parenting, be patient with them. If your friends fail, be patient with them. If your spouse fail, be patient with them. God does it for you all the time and He expects you to do the same.

Remember the woman at the well. Jesus knew how dark her life was. She had been with so many men and the one she was with was not even her husband.

She even looked down on Jesus and the beliefs of the Jews, but Jesus knowing all these things, He still gave her a chance to drink of the water from the well that never runs dry. When He was done with her, she ran and evangelized in the whole community saying, *"Come, see a Man who told me all things that I ever did. Could this be the Christ?"* John 4:29.

The village came to see this Man who had talked to a loose woman like that and did not leave her feeling judged. The people even believed, not because of what the woman said but because they heard the Lord speak to them. The Lord had patiently listened to the woman going on about worshipping, the issues the Samaritans have with the Jews and so on, but Jesus wanted her to recognize who He was and be saved. God waits patiently for you to come to Him girl, and be saved from all that which troubles you, not just sins.

Love is kind. Girl Child, if you keep on accepting abuse and insults and say that person loves you because he buys you flowers, then you have not met up with love. I know you may be saying, you are exercising patience, but sweetheart, that is not love. You see, love is a combination of all these things that the scripture above talks about. That person needs to first meet Christ and receive of His love so he can know what love is.

You girlfriend are not showing love if you are not showing kindness to your friend. Certain things just flow out of the mouth and you wonder how filthy the heart is wherefrom they come. Say kind things, do kind things to others, show love in what you do and receive love back. God has showed us the greatest kindness by sending His One and Only Son to die for our sins, we did not deserve that. Spread some love to others girl, and make this place a better place for us all.

We as girls struggle a lot with envy. I want what my friend has or better. I want a better house than hers. I will buy better shoes than her. She cannot drive a better car than me. Oh, my husband is better than hers, he earns more, and he preaches better than hers, he has a better job. Sounds familiar, be honest baby girl! More and more, debts upon debts, frustration upon frustration, why, because she can't be better than I am.

Remember John the Baptist? He was the one who leaped in his mother's womb when Jesus' mother came to visit. He is the one that came before Jesus and shouted in the wilderness, *"Make straight the way of the Lord."* John 1:23. He is the one that told people that they needed to repent and be baptized, and that the Lord was coming. He became famous, whether accepted as good or bad. People came and were baptized.

He of whom John spoke about came. You see, Mary was

a cousin to Elizabeth, this made John and Jesus relatives. They must have played together many times, but when the appointed time came for Jesus Christ to emerge and begin His ministry, John had to make way. Jesus however, did not just come and bulldoze. Jesus came to be baptized by John first and foremost. Jesus did not envy what John was doing. He was comfortable in His own ministry to the point that when others began to compare them saying Jesus was baptizing more people, Jesus withdrew from that place.

But, John the Baptist, with all the years he had been entrusted with telling about the Christ who was coming, all the crowds he had already amassed, he just said, *"This is He of whom I said, 'After me comes a Man who is preferred before me, for He was before me.'"* John 1:30 he also said, *"He must increase, but I must decrease. He who comes from above is above all, he who is of the earth is earthly and speaks of the earth. He who comes from heaven is above all."* John 3:30-31.

There was no competition between the two. They both had their own assignments on this earth. John's assignment was important, yet Jesus was more exalted above John. You see child of God, love does not even parade itself, the Bible says. Jesus did not need to parade Himself to prove Himself better than John. His time had come and John had done his part. Jesus was exalted and John was beheaded, his time was done on earth. Jesus was exalted by the works He did more than the words He said. People could begin to see and say, "He is the prophet", "He is the Messiah", and Peter said "You are the Christ, the Son of the Living God".

It was not envy against John nor was it self-exaltation that made Jesus who He was, it was God. He said of Jesus, *"You are my beloved Son, in You I am well pleased."* Luke 3:22.

Jesus did not need anyone else to prove He was the Son, God said it and they heard it.

God has an assignment for you. God has a husband for you. God has a house for you. God has your children, they are not with Penina or Elkanah, they are with God. Do not look at what others have and want it, appreciate what they have and ask God to give you what He has in store for you. It may be that you are not meant to be well-known like others, but be the best that God has made you and you will make an impact in your own space.

Your boasting Girl Child should be in God, not in yourself. You are not your own, but you are of God. When you boast about yourself, you can fade away in no time, but God is endless and is limitless, there is so much in God you cannot finish Him. Why boast about what is finite, instead of the infinite provision of God.

Love is not puffed up. You did not achieve by your own self, but because of God. There are those people who would study for years and die on their graduation day. What boasting do they have? All the years of studying cannot be shown. May God grant peace to their families. You see daughter of God, no matter how powerful you think you are, you breathe because God put His breath on you. The alarm clock cannot raise a dead man, no matter how much it snoozes and rings again.

Girls have bad tendencies of looking down on others. Some have the nerve of saying their husbands are better than other people's husbands. Before you know it girlfriend, that man could die tomorrow and you will be left with nothing. Praise God every day for what you have and know it comes from Him, knowing that there is more where that came from.

Remember Job, he was wealthy, had sons and daughters. God boasted about Job and Satan dared Him. God can only boast about Himself, for He is over all things and people.

He knew He had put His Spirit on Job and that Job could hold on even in the midst of trouble. Job lost everything but He still remained saying: *"blessed be the name of the Lord."* Job 1:21. He knew all he had was from God and He never ran short. In the end, he got more than he had in the beginning once his troubles were ended. He was wealthier than at first. He had no reason to boast for all he had was from God. Stop boasting Girl Child and bless God.

If you are the kind that vomits words out of your mouth you must know that it smells foul and it is not a loving act. Being rude is never good, and nothing good comes from it.

There are countless times where I have been mistreated and I felt like saying something bad but the words could not form out of my mouth. The funny thing is that I would only find the right rude words after I moved away from the presence of those that made me angry. In my mind I would say these words, but, they would not hear them. Even at the office, I have been made to be so angry to the point of tears, but I would still struggle to find the words on time. It feels stupid, I know, but I would rather be a fool for God, than be a rude person.

Words spoken reach the ears of a person and remain there. Only God is capable of covering our sins, and not remind us thereof. Our minds will always remind us what the other person said to us, especially if it was hurtful words. To some people it is joyful to speak rudely to others, they think they have sorted you out, but that is not love in the eyes of God. Come on, girl, you are bigger than that. You are of your Father who is always kind. You see, even in His rebuke, God is not rude.

Be in your right position child of God, you are royalty, you are kind and always calm and collected.

Daddy's girl, better sit up and listen. Your tendency of

wanting your own things and your own will above all is not loving. I have personally struggled with that to a certain degree. I have always believed that I am always right, why, because I am smart, intelligent, I think before I act, blah blah blah. So, I always had a reason to argue with my husband.

If I wanted this, it was because I thought it through and therefore it was the best thing. Until my husband told me, 'you see Carol, even if you may think that you are right, you must also know that this hurts me. It is not always about you being right, it is also about how I feel about it!' That did it, slowly I began to see it.

Let me tell you what happened one time. My husband always told me that I have this bad habit of leaving things lying around. Of course, somehow I never saw it as a big issue. He told me countless of times not to leave the cellphone charger on the plug. One day, I sent my son to fetch me the cellphone from the plug, he went and fetched it and left the charger there. My husband came in and got a bit irritated, but as calm as he could be, he told me that I still left the charger in the plug. You see, I still do not see what harm a charger can have when it is left in the plug, but he does, and worse, it was left on his side of the bed. (Yes, we do have our own sides).

I argued my point, it was not me but my son. It was actually true, but he was not buying it. I had done it many times, it would not make any difference if it was Lifa who did it or me. He probably learned that from me anyway. I argued until a point where I heard myself saying, "That is unnecessary". I froze a bit, did I say that to him?

Did I actually belittle his issue? I looked at his facial expression and realized that I actually did not utter the words. That was the Holy Spirit talking within me. I was so sure I

15

said it and was waiting for an angry answer. He kept quiet, I kept quiet. I realized that the argument was over, the Lord had spoken, and this was an unnecessary argument. I left the room and the argument ended.

This is typical Girl Child behavior. I want my way or no way. This is wanting your own way above all others. This is being selfish and self-centered. It is not loving at all as you put yourself before others and make yourself a better and more important person than others. Jesus had a choice of remaining in heaven as God, but He chose to come down lower than angels.

Remember, they even came and tended to Him after He fasted for 40 days and nights, He was hungry and was tempted by the devil. He was before them and above them but had come down below them and needed to be tended to by them. He allowed mere men to hammer nails in His hands and feet and made Him feel excruciating pain, just for you and me.

Come on child of God, surely you can get off your high horse and humble yourself. See others as good people just by themselves. You, as who you are, and them as they are. Our assignments are different, but we all belong to one God. Let God be glorified through your action Girl Child.

The one thing God has saved me from in my lifetime is seeing catfights or fights in general. I am the one that always comes after the incident. I also get the story as news that has happened. It has probably helped not to get used to fighting. Love is not easily provoked. It is not easily angered really.

There are people who will get angry simply because the queue is way too long and the person at the counter is too slow. That can be uncomfortable, I don't like standing for too long either, but, some people can really shout at the person behind the counter simply because they are tired of standing for too long. Some people are quick to send a fist in the opposite direction. Girls will take off their shoes and hit the other person. Worse even when they are fighting for a man. Put your anger away, do not let it control you Daddy's girl. You are more beautiful when you are peaceful and calm than when you are angry.

It is expected of you baby girl to do things right all the time, just as your Father in heaven does. Jesus said, I do as My Father does. God hates wrongdoing, He expects us to do the same. You cannot enjoy committing the same mistake over and over, making it a habit and saying you are full of love.

In all things, God is saying, have a positive attitude, a positive impact and live life positively. This will always rub off on the people around you. They will know you as the calm, truthful, patient, kind person who is like God. That is because you are the split image of Your Father. He expects you then to be and to act like Him, not just look like God and yet act like the devil.

God does not expect us to do things that are impossible. Jesus came in the flesh and experienced all these things. He had a chance to be impatient but He chose not to. He had a reason to be angry with the people who were sinful, but He chose to love us all.

Yes, He whipped the people at the temple, He showed them how serious He took His Father's house, but check out that scripture, when He was done, there were no injured or dead people, and Jesus went on to heal the sick immediately afterwards. That does not sound like an angry person. He is just, and expects us to do the same to others, then we will be a replica of God on this earth.

The Bible puts it clearly, *"In this the love of God was manifest-*

Dear Girl Child

ed toward us, that God has sent His only begotten Son into the world, that we might live through Him." 1 John 4:9.

Love manifest, it acts, it does not only take but gives. The kind of giving that is love is sacrificial. It is like giving your best coat to a friend who has none, not your old rags so you can feel good about yourself. It is spending time with your sick friend instead of going to watch a movie. It is taking care of your parents even if they did not manage to take you through school. It is in respecting your husband even if you are more educated than he is or you earn more than him. It is in feeding the poor. It is in thinking of others instead of yourself, for the needs of others. It is in giving others a chance instead of wanting to shine all the time. It is in recognizing the talent in others and not thinking of yourself as better than others.

Love is, kind, good, gracious, merciful, giving, respectful, love is all good things.

Spread some love girl, you have it in you!

3

Appreciate yourself

Beautiful one, the special design of God, the one who was made last and best, yes you Girl Child. Look at yourself in the mirror, you are a masterpiece, not just a piece, but a master piece. God had all the time in the world to make all the other creatures and could benchmark and see that there is something missing in all of them. He took Adam's rib and made a better version of man, and she was called woman.

You see, every part of your body is designed with a specific purpose, and so are you as a whole being. As a young girl, you may not have the hips and big bums. As you enter puberty, the curvaceous signs emerge. The boobs show up, the figure is shaped nicely. Look at it, if you know how, you can hold a baby on your back and they sit nicely on the back. There is shape and it is beautiful.

However, Girl Child, you are not shaped the same as the next girl. She may have more hips than you, but you have beautiful legs. She may have bigger breasts than you and even suffer from back pain whilst you are wallowing in self-pity because of your smaller breasts. These are very simple things you may be saying, but there are many girls who have gone on a hunger spree because they want to look like super models.

You see, to be slim is good, I am working on that too, but to be healthy is the best thing.

Doctors would first want to check if I have high blood pressure or I am diabetic or any of the diseases that are associated with women who are bigger in size.

There is a downside to being overweight, which is the sickness that hangs around because of the fat, but I have tried the starvation part and it does not work, gets me so hungry, angry, short-tempered, sleepy, and just plain not feeling well. I have a desire to lose weight and stay at a good weight level, but starvation is not the way to go.

I do not want to lose weight because of being hung up on how some model look. I do not desire to be a model or to look like one. I have beautiful curves and bums and a figure to go with that. I am fearfully and wonderfully made, great is the works of the hands of God. Great body to behold, beautiful legs that I used to hide until a neighbor exclaimed how beautiful they were and I lost the long dresses.

My sister, get healthy, get well and do it for yourself and not because of others. Do it because it is good for you. Do it in a healthy way as well. Today, there are names for sicknesses associated with people who are trying to lose weight, bulimia and anorexia. These are illnesses, people unable to control themselves in their quest to lose weight.

It all starts with the thought and the desire to lose the weight. If there is low self-esteem, you may begin to compare yourself with others and strive to be like them. Over time, this becomes an obsession and it is dangerous. With all the yo-yo diets, your system can get all messed up. Be healthy, be moderate, and give yourself a chance to lose the weight in a way that is not dangerous to your health.

On the other side, in the quest to deal with the downside of obsessing about losing weight, there are the ones who care less about how much they break the scales.

Without wanting to make you feel bad and look down on yourself, taking good care of yourself is good for you. A 'don't care' attitude can get you to a bedridden state. Imagine the embarrassment of having medical personnel coming to break the door and carrying you on a stretcher because you are so big and sickly you can't even move yourself. I still don't even attempt to look down on such people as there could be an underlying cause, it can be frustration or some imbalance.

However, before you get to that state, would you appreciate yourself to the point of taking care of the body God has given you. Would you try and make good choices. Yes, fun is good, too much fun tips the scales on the wrong side and becomes negative over time. Appreciate the body you have, the family you have and take good care of yourself.

Appreciating yourself goes beyond just taking care of your body. You have way too much to offer girlfriend, the world has not seen your potential yet. You have so much potential that history can be written about you, if you can begin to appreciate who you are and what you have.

Let us look at King Saul of the Israelites. When Samuel first told him that he was the chosen person to lead the people of Israel, he did not think of himself as worthy to take up such a high position. He was the youngest in his family, of the smallest tribe of Benjamin. There was nothing in him that told him it was possible to lead the nation. He had all negativity in his mind to an extent that even after Saul had anointed him he still did not accept his position. When he had to be anointed in front of the people, Saul went to hide. They had to look for him, just imagine how foolish he looked. They had to inquire of the LORD further in order to get to Saul, there he was hiding among the equipment.

For goodness sake, the man had already been anointed by Samuel with oil, but he still kept himself hidden among the equipment.

This was as if he was waiting for everyone to be sure and convinced that he was the chosen one, then he would be convinced. He ascended the throne and fought many battles and won them. The LORD was with him and he became famous, but Saul still lacked confidence, to the extent that he disobeyed God twice. He feared men more than he feared the LORD.

Firstly, he made a sacrifice which was not his responsibility to do in the first place, it was Samuel's. He was afraid he was losing control as his men were becoming despondent in the face of the enemy. Instead of trusting that God would still deliver them even with a few men that remained, he did what was wrong in the eyes of the LORD.

He was given a second chance and he messed that one up as well. He kept the fattened animals and the king from the enemy's camp which God had said they must all be destroyed.

Saul had no confidence in himself and his God. He did not think he had it in him to hold together the army of Israel without giving in to their influence. He lost favor with God and a new king was anointed. However, God did not take the kingdom from him.

Saul continued being king and still fought some battles, he won some, however he lost confidence over the young man, David. As the people sang, Saul killed his thousand and David killed ten thousand, this became an issue for Saul. He was no longer happy being king, he did not want to be king whilst other people were praising David. It was not David that caused Saul to loose favor with God, it was his own doing.

Some women will shout at their husband so much about other women to the extent that a man feels that home is not such a nice place to be. The Bible likens such a woman with a leaking roof, drops of water coming down, drop after drop. If you are still not married girl, may you not be a troublesome wife. If you are already, tone down lady, give that man space to breathe. Let your home be a peaceful place.

Do not view yourself negatively as that will influence your behavior and affect people around you. Appreciate yourself, who you are and what you have to offer in this world. You see, there is only one kind of you in this whole planet since the earth began and there will never be anyone like you. If you do not appreciate yourself, you rob us of knowing you, but you try to offer us what is already there. You are not David girl child, you are Saul, be comfortable with that.

David was comfortable with being anointed king and waited his turn to the point where he did not jump at opportunities to kill King Saul who was standing between him and the throne. David knew he was king, and the rest he left it to God.

When you do not appreciate yourself, sin stands at the door like in the story of Cain.

God told him that, remember that after they made their offerings, Abel with the first of his flocks and Cain with an offering from his produce. Cain did not understand why God appreciated the offering of Abel, God told him, if you do well I would also appreciate you, but sin knocked at the door, and Cain opened the door and the end of it was the death of Abel at the hands of Cain.

Do not let low self-esteem drive you to sin against God.

Girls can go to the extreme in trying to make themselves look better than others, especially when it comes to men. No, Girl Child, you are special in your own right, to run after a man and fight off any girl you see him walking with is wrong. You are way too precious to be spreading rumors about your sister simply because she has done better than you. Appreciate her and yourself, and you may find that there is something good inside of you that the world awaits to enjoy.

As you ascend the boardroom, you would expect that the learned sisters would know better, but shame has not stopped girls from fighting for positions and the attention of men even in the office. Well, as a child of God, that should not even be a matter for consideration, right? You have a priest appointed for you by God, and as royalty, you await with grace for him to come your way.

However, your gracious composure should not be concerned about men in the office, you have your brains to offer in the office not your body. Let the people appreciate your ability and capability in as far as the job is concerned rather than your looks. Appreciate the skills God has deposited in you and stop wanting to be the favorite of the boss as he may begin to expect favors that are beyond work.

You see child of God, people must see God in you even in the office or your workplace. Let's look at Deborah for instance. It is said that she was a prophetess, a wife and a judge. She had these roles because God had deposited in her the ability to handle and excel in all of them. She was able to lead the people to war, even to the point of elevating another woman, who won the war even though Deborah went.

She led Israel, and yet we are not told whether she was beautiful or not.

There is absolutely nothing wrong with being beautiful, and it must be appreciated. However, she did not need beauty to become a prophetess, she just had to hear from God and speak to the people. She did not require looks to judge the people as it is not a prerequisite; she needed to know the law of God.

In the church, amazingly, girls, we have a lot to deal with. What's with you trying to impress the Pastor so much? Did you come to church for the Pastor or to fellowship with brothers and sisters? Pastors' wives are having it even harder because they are seen as less important, the Pastor has the anointing. You see, that wife has already been appointed to the position of wife, leave her alone. Appreciate her role in taking care of her husband and take care of yours or wait for your own if you are not married.

These days, we have Pastors being younger and younger, even single, with girls falling over themselves to prove they are worthy to have his ring on their fingers. There can only be one wife for the Pastor and his eyes will lead him to her, his heart will confirm, his spirit will agree and God will bless that union. You will remain there looking like a fool. No child of God, you don't go to church to look for a husband, a husband will find you baby girl.

Now that the men issues are out of the way, let us talk about our gifts. Who told you, Daddy's girl, that since you are a woman, you cannot serve? Was it Paul? Are you still stuck up on the traditions of the Jews that you have missed the fact that the Spirit of God has been poured out on all flesh already. Many moons ago, He descended in the upper room where Peter, John and all the apostles were, so was Mary, the mother of Jesus, and the other women who followed Jesus. Jesus spoke about the Spirit of God and told us that He will guide us into all things. He said we shall receive power when the Holy Spirit has comes upon us.

What is the point of having gifts if you cannot use them?

He did not give some men to be apostles, prophets, evangelists, teachers and preachers. He gave some, period. He who descended upon the men and women at the upper room, gave gifts to the church. He has a purpose for the gifts and the outpouring of the Spirit of God. He cannot be dormant simply because we cannot determine whether we are in the new or old dispensation.

Even of old, Prophetess Deborah led in the spiritual things as well as government in Israel. She led men to war and won battles against their enemies. Who said a woman cannot rule? Yes, Paul had issues to address with certain churches, with women who were misbehaving and embarrassing their husbands, but that has not drawn women back to the kitchen barefoot and pregnant, you can do that at your own will and pleasure. When the Spirit of God has descended, you will do more than that, for He is like fire, shut up in your bones. Oh, the fire will catch you, you will run around trying to find an outlet.

Work with the Lord, accept your calling, and appreciate the gift in you. Believe me, I started somewhere there. I desired the gifts of the Spirit, but the ones that could work without even a title attached to it. I coveted the gifts of healing so much. I laid my hands on people in the streets, even the crazy ones came to greet, and I would run, but when God called me, I did not expect the office of an Apostle. That was way too out of my league. It worked against a lot of earthly principles. Would I be accepted? What would my husband say really, me, an Apostle?

This discussion came to a point where the Lord told me that I was like a woman whom He married and she still refused to take the surname of her husband.

I was willing to work in the background, put away the title and do God's work, but how would people take the Apostolic Ministering if they did not know I was an Apostle? Anyway, God has a way of putting me into a nice corner, maybe I put myself there and He decided it was the right time.

There are women who arise and begin ministries in areas where there are no men interested in the things of the Lord. Could the gospel be limited because we girls are not confident enough to stand in the high offices? We did not create them, we just opened ourselves to receive the Spirit of the Lord. Anyway, even so, like the Lord said to Jeremiah, before I formed you, I knew you and called you to be a prophet to the nations.

Appreciate yourself and the gift in you girl, the world awaits for powerful, power filled girls, who are sold out for the Lord.

4

Believe God

Some of the things that you have to go through in life are so inconceivable, they are sometimes downright impossible. They do not make sense and you cannot even explain them to someone else. You just have the word and you take it as it is and wait for its fulfillment.

A woman carries a child for over nine months believing that there is life inside. When the baby kicks, she is convinced that indeed she is carrying something that is living, but she can only know for sure when she delivers the baby. The fact that she cannot see the baby will not stop her from buying baby clothes. These days with scanners, you are even told if it will be a boy or a girl. You go out and buy the correct clothes for the unborn child unless the doctor did not see properly. That is easy, proven over the years since Eve was created and she had her first child.

The mind is created to reason things, to check and be convinced of the existence and the truth of a matter. The spirit on the other side believes even without seeing. There is the inner witness that tells you to believe a thing even when you do not see it. Scientists will require proof first and that is the problem of the atheist. Yet they will believe they have brains that they have never seen.

Where am I getting to, Girl Child? There are many things that you have to believe without seeing them and wait in anticipation for their fulfillment.

If you call yourself a child of God, then you are my sister, we both await the coming of the Lord Jesus. Why? Because the word of God says so.

We do not see God walking with us daily as with Adam, God is Spirit and we interact with Him at spiritual level. Unlike a baby, which is physical even though unseen whilst in the womb of the mother, with God, there is nothing physical, except when Jesus came in the flesh and became a living being.

The importance of believing in God as His child my sister is simple, you expect what He has promised. You see, if you are not expecting money, even if I can take it before you receive it, it does not matter to you. Why, because you are not expecting it, you will not claim it back from me, you will not come after me and demand it. It was never yours as you never recognized, perceived and owned it. A mother who goes into a hospital to deliver a baby, even if she passes out in the process, when she wakes up she wants to see her baby. She is expecting the baby, she has believed that a baby is coming.

Could we at least exercise that faith also when it comes to the things of God which we do not see? Expect it, own it even before it comes, give it a name, prepare for it as a mother prepares baby clothes and baby room. When it is delivered, demand it as a mother would forget the labor pains or even the operation and just want to behold her baby.

Some of the people in the Bible were expected to believe the unbelievable and to hold God to His promises. It did not matter to them if this was an impossible thing, God said it, they had to believe it and expect it.

So if the enemy were to steal it, they would go back to He who promised, and say, you promised, therefore I want it.

Take Sarah for instance. God spoke to Abraham six times telling him that He would make him a father of nations. Abraham took the word, left his country to the place God promised. He was 75 years old when he left. In all these six times, he was already old and getting even older. On the 24th the year of that promise, God then spoke to Abraham in the hearing of Sarah. Abraham was already 99 years old and Sarah was 90 years old. They were both very old. At that age, the normal functions were dead already, no hope of a baby. The Bible says Abraham believed God, I guess it is also because God knows the heart.

During their waiting period, Sarah who was known to be barren, came to the point of substitution. It was a point that said, did God really say I will have a child and carry it in my womb? Could Abraham not have a child by another woman? That would still mean the same thing right? God said He would make Abraham a Father of many nations. Abraham had only one wife. It was logical that it would be a child by Sarah, but Sarah being too old to carry a baby, thought of a substitute. She had her maid to have a child by Abraham. That in her own eyes would fulfill the word of God, Abraham would have a child.

God had not planned for a substitute mother for the son He had promised Abraham. He had spoken a word and that word was going to come to pass. Ishmael came, and they watched him grow. Sarah already had an issue with her substitute that she had initially chased Hagar when she was pregnant. Do not bring a substitute child of God, it will give you problems, all the time. Rather have none than settle, because you will never enjoy a substitute.

When Abraham was 99 years old, the Angel of the Lord came and told him that Sarah would have a child by him. Did God have to wait that long, really? Did she have to be old and wrinkled before she could carry a baby? Sarah laughed. It was impossible. She had accepted that she would not have a child for Abraham, he already had a son Ishmael. She could not perceive that God is greater than her imagination could take her.

Be honest child of God, would you wait for 25 years and still believe when you are 90? I think sometimes we think of Sarah as a non-believer. Abraham had also at some point laughed at the idea, that he and his wife would have a child in their old age. This required acceptance of a matter as truth even if everything else points to it being an impossible thing.

It was only after this matter was settled with Sarah that she conceived a child. All these times she had only heard Abraham talking about this matter, but on the seventh time, she heard it herself, the Angel of the Lord spoke in her hearing. Though she laughed, she took the word after she was assured. In a year's time, Isaac was born. An old woman, had a baby.

God said it, it was true and it came to pass.

Look around you girlfriend, what is impossible for God to do for you and through you. He says He will grant you the desires of your heart. Only He can put a desire that He is prepared to give you anyway. He says, no good thing will He withhold from you.

When a guy proposes to a girl, she has to believe that he loves her, and secondly that he will be true to his word and marry her in the near future. Man has been proven a liar, unlike God, he can promise and not fulfill. Yet, you accept the proposal and begin with plans.

Sadly, some have been left at the pulpit wearing a white dress in front of relatives and friends. However, our God is not a son of man, He does not lie.

At least the matter with Sarah had some level of possibility. She was a woman and he was a man, and by some chance, she could still conceive. Well, we all know it was not a chance, it was God's plan. Let's look at Mary the mother of Jesus. She was a virgin betrothed to Joseph. They were not yet married, they were planning the big day. An angel came and told her she would be with child. That was good because she was about to get married, but the angel said she would not need a man for her to have a baby, the Spirit of the Lord would overshadow her and a baby would come as a result.

For Mary, in her days, that was absurd, how can she come up with such a lousy 'lie' like that? I can imagine Joseph thinking, could you not come up with a better explanation? Could you not say you were raped or something. Girl, you better tell the truth! There is no such thing as having a child without a man playing a part. That was Mary's story and she stuck to it. She had no other explanation except what she was told. She began expecting a child, she saw her tummy rise, and she knew it was true, but what kind of child was this, conceived without the seed of a man.

What would people say? What would Joseph and his family say?

How would she explain the shame and embarrassment of getting herself pregnant before meeting with Joseph and then say it was the Spirit of the Lord? Mary had availed herself to the Lord, *"Let it be to me according to your word."* Luke 1:38. That was settled, the consequences were for God to deal with.

It took a visit by an angel in a dream for Joseph to be convinced that Mary was telling the truth. She was having a baby, Joseph was expected to take her as his wife and take care of the miracle baby. That settled their issue, Joseph became the father to Jesus and raised him up.

You may have had a word from the Lord, maybe the word seems unbelievable, maybe the word has tarried way too long such that you think it will not happen. The people in the upper room that waited for the outpouring of the Spirit were only 120. Jesus had said the disciples must tarry in Jerusalem. Where were the multitudes that Jesus fed with a few loaves and fish? They had given up and went home and they did not receive the Holy Spirit on His first grand entrance.

You will miss out on opportunities in life because of unbelief. You will get substitute things because you cannot wait. They will frustrate you and you will not be happy. Why don't you start believing God for your Godly spouse?

It is time that the things God said are held close to our hearts and we wait in anticipation for them. Some are called but don't believe the word of God, they tell you all the encounters but don't come to a point of acceptance.

Believe God, if He has spoken the word, He will see it through. Do not let circumstances make you to have unbelief.

Believe God.

5

Strength within

Life may have thrown its punches at you daughter of the Most High God. You may have already faced hurtful circumstances that made you love life less. It may even seem like you are the only one who has been hurt so much. It may seem like everyone else has it all, but you have been given strength within you to endure and come out triumphant from whatever situation you face.

The girl you see with a broad infectious smile, she has found a way to deal with the hurt and decided that life was worth living. Her joy is not subject to what other people have done to her. She is not sitting in expectation for the world to give her joy, she takes her joy from the Lord.

Her smile is not saying 'all is perfect', No! She has faced even more bad things than you can imagine, but she came to a point of not allowing a situation to continue haunting her forever. She will not let people and situations dictate how she should live her life.

Many girls have been violated, abused and left bleeding. Bleeding from the heart with no-one to wipe off the tears from their faces. Some have been raped by people close to them, people they trusted. Some would not even have the strength to tell others. Mothers have been known to not believe their daughters at times when they tell of what has happened, yet some mothers arise and fight for their daughters.

Dear Girl Child

The story of violation remains in the mind of that girl. She sees the perpetrator, she smells his sweat, and she hears his voice, but you see, she had to move away from the presence of the person who hurt her into the presence of God, for only He can wipe the tears off her face, whisper words of hope in her ears, fill her with everlasting joy and peace.

You have assumed that every other girl has a perfect life. You have compared yourself with others and concluded that yours is not worth living, but child of God, it is your Father who should determine what happens with you. Even after other people have done what is despicable in your life, God has deposited strength in you to endure and to come out of it. There is nothing much we can do about the lawlessness in society. We can only pray for God to save us from encountering them.

It is true that what the other person has done to you is painful. It is true that you still remember it clearly or vividly even if you have moved a distance away. What good is that memory child of God? Yes your mind reminds you of it, but are you continuously meditating on it? Meditating on the thing that hurts you, as if it happened yesterday, will not help you one bit. It will unfortunately keep you in bondage to an act committed by someone who is living their life without a care in the world.

Some matters, Girl Child, are of choice. You can remain pinned down by the enemy or you can arise and refuse to be kept down and under. You can choose to take the punches or you can walk away. You can choose to fight back with the armor of God or roll down and play dead. The enemy will keep on trampling you until he destroys you, unless you take your position, fully armed and win the battle. This is a battle that is in your mind, where you have to constantly erase the lies of the enemy.

Precious one, do not let the enemy lie to you telling you that you are at fault. He will try and tell you that you were not supposed to wear that short skirt, you attracted that beast. If that were true, then babies who are fully dressed even with disposable nappies, are not in any way a sexual attraction, and should not be violated. They are not dressed up to attract such acts. The mind of a beast is on finding its prey, whether dressed for the occasion or not. At the beach, most people are exposed also, you don't see the beasts running after every beautifully figured girl simply because they see the parts that are normally covered. So, no, it was never your fault.

Think back on the story of Gideon in the Bible. The Israelites were defeated and scared of their enemies. There was no hope for a better life. Their produce was stolen from them all the time. This was to a point where Gideon had to hide the produce so he and his family did not starve. They were totally defeated and harassed by the enemy.

The Lord came and told Gideon that he was a mighty man of valor. There was nothing visibly mighty about Gideon, he was scared to the core. He was not able to stand up against the enemy, he did not know how. I know this is nothing closer to the violation of your physical body, but God said to Gideon he must go fight with the strength he had. So, this man had strength to fight the enemy, yet he cowardly hid the produce not knowing he was the answer to Israel's woes.

You do not need ten girls to sit around on the floor crying with you, making you feel even more miserable. You do not need pity-parties, what you need is a reminder from God that you have strength within you. You need the assurance from God that this too shall pass. You need to know the power that is already within you to defeat the enemy. It is a mindset shift, change your thinking to the positive.

The enemy is not as strong as you think, you give him too much credit.

Paul said *"that I may know Him and the power of resurrection, and the fellowship of His suffering…"* Philippians 3:10. He recognized that there is a greater power in operation, the power that raised Jesus. Jesus was not called out of the grave, He came out of the grave. All the people that had been raised before, needed a human being to call them out of death to life, to plead for them for God to give them life again. Jesus did not need anyone but the Spirit of God, the invisible power of creation raised Him up.

You are well and able, precious daughter of God to stand up against the issues that trouble you. The people in the Bible were just as human as you and I. Remember Deborah, the prophetess, judge and wife? When the head of the army feared going to the battle without Deborah, she stepped in. How can a man want a woman to accompany him to a battle?

Yet this man knew that there was a power within Deborah, the power that set her up as a ruler in Israel. The power that spoke through her for the nation. This power would be essential for the battle at hand. Deborah went with them, the Bible does not say she killed people. The most troublesome person Sisera was killed by another woman, Jael.

The presence of Deborah in the battle gave them victory over the enemy. Deborah had already declared before they went to battle that it would be won by a woman. She did not have inferiority complex issues. She was sure of her position and was prepared to give space for another woman to take the position and win the battle.

The power in you may not be to do the actual battle yourself. You will be required to submit yourself to God for Him to work out a great miracle in your life.

Your problem, Girl Child, is that you want to always do it yourself. You want to show people that you have everything covered, that you are in control. There are situations that require you to lift a hand and do something, yet some things require you to stand and see the victory given by the Lord to you.

God has deposited strength and ability to influence in you. You are the change that you want to see in your life and around you. You are not a beaten up, powerless and hopeless person. The Bible says, *"Yet in all these things we are more than conquerors through Him who loved us."* Romans 8:37. You can beat the fear, the low self-esteem, the bitterness, the anger and just about everything that is pulling you back.

When Moses gave all the reasons why He could not go and save the people, God reminded him that He is the one who made the mouth which he was going to use, to speak to Pharaoh. You would think God would have given instructions to go and battle it out with Pharaoh, but no, God did not tell Moses to go and fight Pharaoh, but to talk to him. Moses went there ten times, and all these times, God raised His hand against the Egyptians, but Moses had to go and do something, say something, raise up his staff or just go and speak to Pharaoh. God was the one who did all the plaques until they were released.

It is the glory of God when His children arise and show the strength of their Father. The power of God is strengthened in your weakness dear child of God. He wants to show His enemies how strong He is. He is above all things, sovereign and mighty in battle. There is no battle too difficult for God. It is only ourselves that move away from God, and trust in our own understanding and strength. Don't fail because you have sought only your strength, be victorious with the strength God has given you.

The world has to know and see the manifestation of the sons of God. Yes, you are a son of God too on this earth that the creation is awaiting. Sons of God will display the traits of their Father. Jesus did not stop doing the work of God simply because the people rejected Him in one area. Even when they wanted to stone Him, when they ridiculed Him, when they tried to trap Him. He showed Himself God amongst them, without any shadow of doubt. They had met a different being, one all-powerful was amongst them and they did not recognize Him.

It was a difficult thing for Jesus to go to the cross. He was a human being and also God, He felt real pain in His body. He went to the cross knowing it would be painful. He could have stopped all that anytime during the process, but He did not. He endured till the end. Mary, His mother could have intervened and pleaded with the people, but she watched as they beat her son, she watched Him at the cross. She also had the strength to endure seeing Jesus suffering like that. In fact, she was already told by Simeon that He was going to suffer.

Do not give up on life because of the challenges you face. Do not stop living because you hurt too much. Don't be a suicide statistic because you can't handle what you are going through. When you are in a valley of death, you have to pass through it, not stop and die in the valley. David knew that he had to walk through the valley, not sit and die in the valley. There is so much that you still have to achieve. The valley is a chance for you to see the power of God. He is with you even through the valley, His rod and His staff is there to comfort you. Lean on God and pull through it.

6

Attitude is key

If the eagle were to think like the other birds, it will only fly to the level of other birds. If the eagle were to mind the power of the wind and the storm, it will go down to earth and find refuge under a shelter, but the eagle has an attitude different from other birds. It recognizes the storm coming, but it also recognizes the ability to fly through and go above the storm. The eagle knows how powerful the storm is and the wind, but it also knows that just above the storm there will be safety. So it flies above the clouds, above the storm.

Your attitude determines how far you can go child of God. How do you see things around you? You can be so miserable in life if you sit down and throw a pity party every time something goes wrong. Some would want everyone to come and sit around listening to what happened, how it happened, when it happened and how she felt, how she cried all night and so it goes, the whole day spent crying with a sister with no solution at hand. After all the tears, the problems still remain. That is so unfruitful.

How do you see a challenge child of God? This will determine how far you will go to resolve it. Challenges are normally man made. Focusing on the person who did it will not resolve the issue, but focusing on the solution to the problem will resolve it.

Remember the famous girl at school, the one you all envied? She had an attitude of being all-important and everyone gave her that space, but that would not give her good grades, would it? It is the hard working person who knows that their straight A's do not come from being famous, but from working hard, studying.

Remember Deborah, her attitude was different from the head of the army. She was not scared of the battle, she went knowing that the battle was already won. She did not even know the woman she said the battle would be won by, she just believed God would give them victory through a woman. If it was you girlfriend, you would have thought of yourself as the most fitting person to win the battle because you are already the judge and prophetess. Deborah knew team work would give them victory.

The 12 spies that were sent by Moses to spy out the land came back with two reports. One group of 10 said the land is flowing with milk and honey, here are the grapes to show how rich the land is, but the people are too big and dangerous. These 10 spies put fear in the hearts of the people for they had an attitude of cowards. They had forgotten how God took them out of Egypt with His mighty hand. They saw the giants as bigger than God who put Pharaoh and his horses and chariots into the Red Sea.

Joshua and Caleb had a different spirit. They also saw the land of milk and honey, they saw the grapes, and they saw the giants, but they remembered that their God is bigger than the giants. They knew that God would not send them to the land and let them be meat to their enemies. God had already invested so much into that nation to let them be destroyed in the land He promised them. They knew that God is faithful, and the word He speaks, He causes it to come to pass.

With the negative attitude of the 10, the people were discouraged and they complained and cried for they saw defeat. God heard their complaints and decided that for the 40 days the spies went to the land of Canaan, the Israelites would spend 40 years in the wilderness. They would not see the Promised Land, all the adults of that generation. Only their children would enter the land. They lost out on the promises, on the brink of it, simply because their attitude was bad.

You need to have an attitude of a winner in life girl. The world is not waiting to give you the best treatment, it is waiting for you to give it the best attitude. An attitude that say, 'I can do this even though it is difficult'.

That is the attitude that takes you to greater heights. That was the attitude of David when he faced Goliath. Goliath saw a small boy, he even insulted him. He was a trained soldier, a warrior, a big one for that matter. He had battled out with adults and experienced soldiers and won. He had already put fear in the heart of Saul the King and all his soldiers. Who was this small boy to even attempt to fight him?

David went to battle without an amour on. With only a small stone David saw Goliath differently. David saw how big Goliath was and how easy it would be for the stone to hit him. David did not consider the spear and javelin that could have hit and killed him, but he considered God of the Armies of Israel. He was determined that the uncircumcised Philistine was not going to speak badly about his God and get away with it. He saw the defeat of the enemy by His God before it happened.

Have a winners' attitude and you will surely become a winner. If you are defeated in your mind, even the smallest wind will take you down.

A positive attitude is not only about winning battles.

Dear Girl Child

You may be in a low paying job that has customers that vomit vile words with their mouths. That can make you hate your job and even give bad service to your customers. People don't know how much you earn and simply don't care. All they know is that they are there to be served by you and you are paid to do that work.

It is disheartening to bring your money to buy something and only to be given a bad attitude by the person who will benefit from the money you bring as a customer. Ladies, even if your husband made you cross in the morning, don't take it out on your customers, they have nothing to do with it.

What about the attitude that says you are the best thing that happened to the company and so everyone must bow to you? That's also a bad attitude. Everyone is important in a company or even at church.

You are in the choir at church, you have a beautiful voice, now everyone must follow your lead.

You can't be best in all songs, even if you were, there is a reason why it is called a choir, it is a team and teams share responsibilities and the stage.

Some of you girls trip over yourselves to get the attention of the pastor. You think you are the best person who has the best interest at heart for the pastor. You even criticize the pastor's wife on how she handles her household as if you can do a better job. Women sleep on wet pillows because of the way they are treated by other women, competing for the attention of their husbands with some girls in church. Girl, get your own man.

Remember Miriam, Moses's sister. She was a prophetess and older than Moses. She was the one who assisted Moses to be safe during the time Pharaoh killed young boys.

She probably had in mind the thought that she saved him and now he has come to be savior for Israel. After all that God had done through Moses, Miriam thought because she also heard from God as a prophetess then she was in the same league as Moses. She said, *"Has the LORD indeed spoken only through Moses? Has He not spoken through us also?"* Numbers 12:2.

That was jealousy creeping in. Who was this Moses, making himself more special than us? If God can speak to Aaron surely He speaks to her as well. Moses was just as human as they were and younger, but God choses His servant, Moses was chosen. God defended Moses in a painful manner. Miriam ended up with leprosy and was out of the camp for seven days. Talk about rejection! She who thought was as special to God as Moses was, ended up in the rejection area, outside the camp, shouting 'unclean, unclean'. That was a bad lesson for those who think they are better than others.

Have a positive attitude, even when you have been blessed amongst your people. The bible says, pride comes before a fall. Your boasting and looking down on people will take you down and no one will be there to help you up. Looking down on yourself also is not good as you will not go anywhere.

You need an attitude that say, *"I can do all things through Christ who strengthens me."* Philippians 4:13.

When you have done it all, you need an attitude that says, I have done it all through Christ who has given me strength. The God that we serve is a jealous God, His glory He will not share with anyone. Allow God to take you to greater heights by His power and be a blessing to others along the way.

Look at life the way God sees it. Look at Jesus, He was fully man on earth, yet He was God.

He left His kingdom in heaven to come down and be lower than the angels. He did not know hunger until He came on earth, not even pain and being weary. He felt all these things on this earth though He had the power to say, 'I will pass on this one', yet He said, *"Oh My Father, if it is possible, let this cup pass from Me, nevertheless, not as I will, but as You will."* Matthew 26:39.

He had an attitude of not quitting, of pressing on. When He was rejected one side, He went to the other and continued preaching the good news. He dined with the sinners and the rich people as well as the self-righteous ones. He did not demand a high office in the temple or synagogue. He went in to do the work of God, selflessly and tirelessly.

His attitude was a positive one, He brought change wherever He was. No matter what His circumstances were. One time He got on a boat after preaching to the multitudes to go rest elsewhere, the people followed Him there and wanted Him to continue preaching to them.

If you are called of God my sister, do not be tired of doing good things. Your reward is in heaven. Even if they may ridicule you and look down on your ministry, your attitude should be that of an eagle, soar high above the winds and the storms. Let God lead you, then you will not fear in the valley for you will know God is with you. When you get victory, you will not think it was just your own doing, but God who works all things together for good for you.

7

Your sisters around you

We have heard it all, 'pull her down' syndrome. We talk about it every time we meet to encourage each other as girls. We know it is not a right thing to do but we do it anyway.

There is a wealth of wisdom and knowledge all around you Girl Child. There are many other girls who have gone through stuff that you can never imagine. There are girls that have a story to tell, one that will leave you thinking that you actually do not have a problem at all. These are sisters who have endured, triumphed and came out of situations victorious. They may not look like your Oprah Winfrey or Joyce Meyer, but they are ordinary women who have done extra ordinary things.

These are the women who have a well of wisdom that can nourish your soul and build you up. They can empower you to achieve your goals. They appreciate a helping hand because they have also received such to be where they are. They do not look down on your challenge but give a testimony that says, 'I have been through worse and I came out triumphant'. They can tell you how they made it and how you can make it.

There is an idiom that says, the road ahead is enquired from those in front. For the one who is at your level is also trying to figure out how to get out of the situation the same as you.

Some of these women may actually be girls still but have gone through the issue you face and can give you advice.

At times, you may feel that telling your story to someone else will expose you and that they will laugh and gossip about you. What if they did? It would not change your situation one bit, but staying with a matter because you can't trust a single person will just cause you depression.

We need each other, we just need more wisdom in identifying the right person to seek help from.

The woman who supported Prophet Elisha and she was given a son who later died knew where to get help. She could have just stayed at home and buried her son, but she was determined to go to the man who had prayed for her to have the son. On her way, she met up with the servant who asked her if all is well, she said all is well. She knew her help would not come from this man. In fact, that man ran home to try and raise up the boy to no avail. Only Elisha was able to raise the boy up by praying to God. She knew she needed an intervention and she was determined to get it.

When Mary heard the news from the angel that she would be with child, and that Elizabeth her cousin also was with child, she arose and went to see her. She was not married but was going to have a baby. She did not need stares from people in the village, she did not need the reprimand of her parents, she needed a like-minded person to rejoice with her.

These are baby-leaping moments when you meet someone who shares the same zeal for success as you do. When Mary greeted, the babe in the womb of Elizabeth leaped. Before Mary could tell her story about the angel, Elizabeth already knew that Mary was the mother of the Savior. She was excited to be greeted by a chosen woman as Mary was.

She did not despise her own babe who was not going to be the Messiah but was going to prepare for the Messiah to come.

Elizabeth had experienced a miracle, she who was barren till her old age had conceived a child. It was not her own strength and effort, she knew that very well. She also knew that the mother of her Lord was blessed and chosen to carry the Lord to this earth. She was not jealous that Mary was carrying the Lord, but she rejoiced with her. Her attitude was a positive one. She did not ask about the marriage between Mary and Joseph. She knew there was a bigger destiny for the two of them.

Mary stayed with Elizabeth for some time. She would not have to explain herself to people concerning her bulging belly.

She just rejoiced in the presence of another blessed woman. Who are you surrounding yourself with?

When you are in the company of girls, does your babe leap? Are you encouraged and empowered or do you just talk about destructive things? When you find girls talking, it is about men and clothes. When you find guys talking, it is about sports and women. Be a different kind of girl, when you meet, let it be a time for the babes to rejoice in the belly as they hear your greetings to your sister. Let there be discussions on how to position the kingdom of God in business, politics, society. Let it be about how to do things better at church.

Girls, you have more to offer to each other than just complimenting each other on the latest and most expensive weaves. You are more than your Brazilian hair, surely you are more than the BMW your husband bought you. You surely are more than the salary you earn.

What will the coming generation say they have learned from this generation? I know there are few women I would like to get close to, to tap into their anointing. To have my babe leaping moments also. For I know there is wisdom to be attained from others.

What about also availing yourself to another girl. These days we have so many businesswomen, are they available for the younger girls to be mentored? It takes time and effort to assist another person who is not of your league in any area. Some of you will say that you have struggled by yourself to be where you are then others must do the same.

Remember Ruth and Naomi. As much as Naomi entreated Ruth to go back to her father's house, she would not budge. She had seen her mother-in-law at home all the years since she got married to that family. She knew that Naomi was from a good nation, from a people with good principles. However, she knew that Naomi had God, unlike the gods of their area. She wanted to be associated with Naomi and not to go back to her father's house to the useless gods.

Ruth went back with Naomi and followed her instructions. She was seen in the village and people spoke about her. She was the daughter-in-law who came back to take care of her mother-in-law. She would not let her go back alone, with no child and no grandchild, who was going to look after her?

Naomi had wisdom and knowledge, she saw the opportunity for the kinsman redeemer to come in to the picture and save them from poverty and marry the young Ruth. She sent Ruth to glean in the field of Boaz, knowing that he will have an interest. Eventually, Ruth was married by Boaz and became grandmother in the lineage of David up to Jesus.

Ruth benefited from surrounding herself with an old woman and not her younger sister who went back to her father's house.

The friends that you have must deposit something that is good in your life or they are not worth it. The ones who will indeed pull you down are the ones who wants to be at the top and look down at you. If you are the one doing the pulling down, then stop that and become a better person. You need people around you, no one lives in isolation of company. You better be good company yourself and be in the company of good people, then you will be empowered.

Reading the book of 1st and 2nd Timothy indicates the kind of friendship that an older man had with a young one, Paul and Timothy. Just like Ruth and Naomi, except that these two were related. Paul had travelled with Timothy to different churches over a number of years. Timothy learned from Paul and at a later stage he was ready to lead the church of Ephesus. The gift in Timothy was imparted by the laying on of hands. Do you have a gift Girl Child? Has anyone laid hands on you? Are you in the right company to grow in the things of the Lord?

Paul exposed Timothy to various church matters and advised him on how to deal with them. That says to me, Paul was not threatened by the young Timothy as we see other leaders today. Older ladies, the young ones need your support and encouragement, but more so your teaching and send-off. When a young person is ready to minister the word of God, it does not mean she no longer needs a mentor.

Don't go off and forget your Naomi baby girl, simply because doors of opportunity have been opened for you. You will still need advice like Timothy needed from Paul.

You need the company of matured women also where you will receive proper guidance and even rebuke. Yes, you need someone bold enough to tell you when you have done something wrong. Sitting around with people who agree with every wrong thing you do may seem fine for a while, but you are all are going down the wrong path with no one to tell you otherwise.

Some sisters want to be the center of attraction all the time. You know those who want you to come to their house and they don't even know the directions to your house. The ones who want you at their party and you must come and help, yet they will be too busy or engaged elsewhere when you throw a party. They are the ones who will not call you when you are sick, but when they are sick everyone must take notice and be around to help out. These still need to learn a lesson from the relationship of David and Jonathan.

Jonathan had every reason to hate David for he was the anointed King in waiting. He was waiting for King Saul to die, the father of Jonathan. Jonathan would have been king after his father if it was not for David who was chosen after the disobedience of King Saul. Jonathan had so much love for David, he even protected him from his father, King Saul, who many times tried to kill David. Now, there is a friend who sticks closer than a brother.

Be the kind of friend who will be dearly missed when you are not there, not the kind that people are glad when they don't see you around in gatherings. When Dorcas died as recorded in the bible, the people of the village wept for her. They brought the things she made for them, clothing and other stuff. She had left a big mark in the lives of the people around her. They had every reason to ask the Apostles to raise her up. They pleaded because they knew how valuable she was to them, she had done many good things for the community.

What kind of a person are you?

Would people do the same if you were to go?

Sisterhood is not just about friendship, but about relation-ships with other girls or ladies. I have met ladies that have made an impact in my life. I do not say these are my talk-to-daily kind of friends, but these are precious people in my life. I am not a demanding kind of friend, but I have been there for my friends and to other people in need.

I appreciate ladies who have done well in life. I am amazed at how women were looked down upon and expected to take the back seat, but are now rising to do amazing things. I appreciate ladies who without being in competition with men, make a mark in society. I want to know how wom-en have been doing it. I learn things from other women, in business, in marriage and in ministry.

I have also met girls who look up to me. Girls who appre-ciate the advice I give them, praying with them. At times I would wonder what the girls see in me, but Daddy reminds me that I have to make an impact on others. The kingdom of heaven expands just like yeast, it grows like a mustard seed.

In each and every one of us, there is a Mary who needs Eliz-abeth at some point in life, one who would share in your joy for she understands the joy of the Lord also. One who will help to incubate the baby in you, be it a business idea, talent, a gift, a calling or whatever the Lord has laid in your heart.

In each and every one of us, there is a Naomi who must lead a kind of Ruth to her destiny. The kind that will not say, "Let me get it for myself first", but will know that there is a greater plan for Ruth and she must assist.

Dear Girl Child

There is a Dorcas in each one of us, one who is supposed to help someone who is poor. Her reward is with God and not with her sisters. She gives without measure and expectation. She understands that *"It is more blessed to give than to receive."* Acts 20:35.   This kind of girl will be remembered by God in her time of need. She will also be remembered by her friends. It is important to remember to be a good friend and to have good friends.

8

The male species

Butterflies in your stomach, broad smile for no apparent reason, taking care of how you look frequently? Is there someone you are trying to impress baby girl? His presence changes your mood immediately, even your posture changes. You are in for it big time. Love is in the air, so they say. You alone smell it as you are the target of interest. A man has come in to mess up with the functioning of your stomach.

It is a good feeling girl to be in love with someone. They occupy your thoughts, you wonder what they are doing when they are not around, and you want them to miss you as much as you miss them. You want to call them so frequently even though you don't have much to say.

I remember when I met my husband. I used to call him and have nothing to say, truly I had nothing to say, just wanted to hear his voice. I remember that I would see him after work and then go home with all goodbyes said, but later in the evening, his car would be at the gate, even though when we parted we agreed to see each other the following day. He would go home and find nothing interesting and then drive to see me again. This was just love, simple. We were older and ready to marry and we did within a few months.

Now, if you are still younger, you may experience the butterflies and think it is love.

Dear Girl Child

You may think the definition of love has something to do with the roses he buys you, the love notes he leaves behind, and the endless calls he makes. He may be giving you so much attention that you think he is all love.

As a young person, ask yourself if you are ready to be married yet?

You see, all these efforts will subside one day as you get used to each other and he no longer wants to impress you. So if you get into a relationship at a young age when you are not yet ready to get married, chances are, when he gets relaxed you will think he no longer loves you. What does he know about love anyway when he is also too young to marry you.

Let's not confuse infatuation and lust with love. The first two are temporary, once satisfied they move on to the next target. Girl, you deserve better than being used as a tester for a boy who is still trying to figure out what's going on inside himself. He has no thoughts of building a house and buying furniture. His thoughts are still on satisfying the fire in his body and you seem to be the water tanker. Once the fire is out, he is also out.

No one buys a lipstick that is written tester from the shop. A tester is just for that, testing, 'How do I look in this lipstick?' After testing, the person may not like that kind of lipstick and would then look for a different kind. They test it and see that it does not look good on them and move on to the next. The tester remains there, just a tester. Once a person has decided on the lipstick they like, they buy the one which is sealed and pay full price for it and leave the tester at the shop.

You are way too precious to be used as a tester child of God. Once a tester is opened, it cannot be resealed, even if it can be refilled. Something will always be missing.

A wife is supposed to be wrapped up for her husband to be unwrapped at the appropriate time. She is to be enjoyed by the one target of her affection for life. When you are tested before, then you are a subject of discussion. 'Oh, I tested the red lipstick, it does not look good on me, it does not smell so good, it is a bit rough on the edge, it wears off too fast, it does not last long…' They are talking about you who has just given yourself up to that boy, and he is telling his friends how you did not meet the scales.

The scars that comes with sexual relations when you are young and unmarried remain for a long time. Let me say this, I was also not perfect. I also went the wrong way. I have regrets that comes with not waiting. I wish certain things could be reversed so I can start again. I wish I had made the right choices all the time.

The good thing about being young and a virgin is that you still have a choice to wait on the Lord. Once that virginity is broken, you can't bring it back. I know that we say you are a new creation, but fact remains, it was broken inside physically at one point in your life and you cannot change that. You can love yourself as a new person, yet the mind will still remind you, more like the devil reminding you what you did before.

It may seem like the 'in thing' to give yourself up. It may seem like you will fit in when you give it up. You may seem like a fool if you don't give it up, but you better be a fool for God, and remain pure, than to please friends at the expense of your relationship with God. The boy will go home, and you will remain with the thoughts. You may even want more and start a cycle of fornication that eventually becomes a norm for your life.

When God says flee from sexual immorality He means just that, flee. You are truly an attractive species baby girl.

56

Dear Girl Child

You have the curves to show off with, you have the protruding chest that makes the boys' knees wobble, and you have the backside that makes them want you more. Sometimes, you flaunt it so well that you are irresistible. Are you for sale child of God? They mostly advertise things that are for sale, mostly stock they want to get rid of in the shop so they can bring new stock. People will run to buy the half-price items, buy one get one free.

No, you cannot be for sale child of God. You have already been bought by the blood of the Lamb. You cannot be sold to anyone, not even for a five course meal at an expensive restaurant. Not even by the latest and most expensive phone. Not even the most expensive car can match the blood of Jesus that bought you. You are not second hand material, you are not second best, and you are the best for Jesus.

Paul said to the virgins, they must give themselves to the work of the Lord. Whilst you wait for your husband to find you, give yourself to the work of the Lord. Be active in church, lend a hand to the older people and the poor.

Be an example to the younger ones, by your conduct. Paul further said to Timothy, *"Let no one despise your youth, but be an example to believers in word, in conduct, in love, in spirit, in faith, in purity."*1 Timothy 4:12.

People must see your conduct and have respect for you. They must see God in your conduct. They must see that in you is the Spirit of God. They then will have nothing to despise you for. More so, when you conduct yourself in a good manner, you are honoring God with your body. He said, *"Be holy, for I am holy."* 1 Peter 1:16.

If you have fallen by the wayside, know that God has a forgiving heart. His arms are always open to a repentant heart. He is there to wash you and cleanse you with the blood of Jesus and make you a new creation. Paul said in Romans 8:1 *"There is therefore now no condemnation to those who are in Christ Jesus, who do not walk according to the flesh, but according to the Spirit."*

Let no one then hold this against you. When you have fallen and Jesus has extended His helping hand, rise up, shake the dust off and receive the forgiveness of the Lord. Jesus came not for the righteous, for they need nothing much from Him, but for the sinners. You are not meant for destruction if you are in Jesus. Go to Jesus, the Bible says, *"Blessed is he whose transgression is forgiven, whose sin is covered."* Psalm 32:1. When Jesus forgives your sins, you are blessed, therefore receive your blessings child of God.

Ready for marriage

There comes a time when the male species seems to be so attractive they seem eternal. That's where you look at him and think 'forever'. You have passed the stage of confusion, you probably have a few scars to show, now you are ready to take the big step. At times it seems like the options are too limited. You have become wiser, your standard has become higher, and you know what you are looking for. Hopefully, you are not hung up in the past and judging the brothers according to whoever hurt you in the past.

Forever is a long time, a life time is a long time to spend with the wrong choice of a person. When you were younger, your interest in boys was different from when you are older. When you are older and ready for marriage, the issues to look for are more serious.

You want sustainability, you want maturity, and you want responsibility and accountability in the prospective husband. The good thing about you Girl Child is that you are the hunted and not the hunter.

Your husband finds you waiting for him and you have the privilege of assessing him for suitability. When you go around selling yourself to men you have missed the plot. Eve did not find Adam, but Adam saw her first, and determined, declared, *"This is now bone of my bones, and flesh of my flesh."* Genesis 2:23. Adam saw in Eve someone who looked like him but was not him. Eve was a compatible companion, not like in the previous attempts where it was written, there was not found a companion suitable for Adam.

A wife is found by her husband. When you go around looking for a husband, you may find those that want to take advantage of your desperation. It is in the man's ego to hunt and find himself a wife. It is your part though, as a woman, to check the brother out. Does he have the qualities you seek for in a husband? Is he born again?

Many girls marry men who are not born again with the idea that they will pray for his salvation. Do not think, child of God that you can change your husband. He is God's creation and only His creator can change him. You will spend a lifetime trying to make your husband who he is not, whilst staying in a miserable marriage. When you get married, you get yoked with that person. You cannot come back later and say he is not your type, he does not suit you, he does not make you happy, or whatever other reason you have about him, when you knew him before you got married.

The word of God says, *"Do not be unequally yoked unbelievers."* 2 Corinthians 6:14. This is a straight forward instruction. Once the cows begin ploughing, there is no time to change the partners as it delays the process.

The animals have to plough together towards the same direction. Marriages fail because the people are not moving towards the same direction.

You may be called to minister and you are married to an unbeliever who does not even believe you are called. You will struggle to do the work of God because your husband, the head of your household does not believe in the same things you do. You may be called in to appease the ancestors if you are married to a traditionalist who still believe in ancestral worship. The whole family will be looking at you to cook and prepare meals for such gatherings whilst your faith does not allow you to do that.

Do not get married out of desperation girlfriend, don't settle for the only available man. Yours is still being prepared. Some will end up unmarried anyway, Apostle Paul said such will give themselves time to serve the Lord. So instead of worrying yourself about getting the right husband, get closer to the Lord. Your husband must find you hidden in God with Christ. It is only the one who knows Christ who will know where to find you.

You are too special to be desperate. He may look good, have the money in the bank, drive a fancy car, promise to marry you tomorrow, but if he is not right for you, don't settle. Don't go in there thinking he will change. Let God change him first and if he is yours he will come back once he has found Christ.

The life we live today is not the same as the olden days where women were expected to stay at home, barefoot and pregnant. Women today have so much to offer. You have a high paying job girl, you are an executive and a very important person at work. When you get home, your husband is the head, and then your mind is not able to get around it.

Let your spirit lead in this case and be renewed in your mind.

You may find that the husband that is right for you earns less than you do. You may find that he is not as wealthy as you are, but he is right for you. Some girls would rather settle for the rich man than marry the right man. The rich man will leave your bed baby girl and go gallivanting with other girls out there. I am not saying all rich men are like that.

I am saying if he was not meant for you, it will not last. You may have all the material things in the world but cannot fill each other's hearts desires. Money cannot be a yardstick for marriage, not even status.

It is exciting for a girl to marry the pastor of the church. It may seem like she won against all the girls who were eyeing him. It may seem like a big achievement, but though he is a pastor, he may still not be the right man for you. If being a pastor made him the right husband, we would not be seeing many divorces of pastors as we see these days.

Marriage is an institution where you enroll sober minded, after having searched yourself and found to be qualifying to enter. It is a lifelong commitment baby girl, divorce does not please God. You may have all the reasons for divorce, it still does not please God. You work hard to keep your marriage, keep the joy, peace and the fires burning.

It is the will of God that you marry and be happy in your marriage. It is your responsibility to accept a marriage proposal from the right man. It is also your responsibility to find out from God if the person proposing is the right man.

Now that you are married

The reality of marriage sinks in within a few weeks of saying 'I do'. If you were the girl that used to take care of yourself only, all of a sudden there is someone who needs taking care of. Let's face it, even with the highest executive job, it is the pleasure of a woman to cook a meal for her husband, and it is the joy of a man to receive such treatment.

You were used to getting up and just going, and suddenly, there is someone who cares about where you are. Some go to the extreme of wanting to know who you are with and what you are doing there. Some want you to ask for permission before you go. If you never talked about these things, the rules of the game, you will be in for a shock of your life. This is a serious adjustment which you may not see in the first few weeks because it is a joy for you to report your whereabouts all the time, you seem to think it is love.

Marriage can really be one of the greatest decision you have taken and some have marital bliss throughout, but for some, you will go through trial and error until you find a comfortable zone in which you will both find your peace and joy.

Think of Sarah (then Sarai) for a while. She got married to Abraham (then Abram). Before long, Abraham said they must get out of his father's place into a land unknown because an unknown God told him to go. What would you do as Sarah? To leave the comfort of your home to an unknown land led by an unknown God. Remember, their family was an idol worshiping people, but Sarah went with her husband.

Their first test of endurance came when the place they were in experienced drought, then they had to leave for Egypt. You and I would have probably given Abraham a piece of our mind. What kind of God gets them out of their home into a land that has drought within a short time? Did you hear well Abraham?

What kind of man is unable to feed his family? However,

Dear Girl Child

Sarah went with Abraham.

In Egypt, Abraham asked Sarah to say he was her brother, she said so and was taken to the palace for the king to take her as his wife. The king did not touch her, but God judged them for Abraham's sake. Today, you would open a case of human trafficking if your husband did the same thing. This happened again and Sarah was again at risk, but they all came out safely. Abraham thought of his own safety and risked the safety of his wife. I am inclined to say he trusted God to take care of his wife.

What would you do lady if you were in her position? She still called him master. She still gave her maid over to have a child by him seeing she was barren. She gave up on having her own son and had to watch Ishmael taking the affection of his father. No wonder when Isaac was born, Sarah demanded that Hagar and Ishmael be sent away. It was too much for her to share Abraham, more so for her son to share his inheritance with the son of a bondwoman.

As a married woman, be careful of the choices you make.

Be sure to find out the will of God concerning your life, your husband and your entire family. Women are known to persevere. Some say if you were to open the roof of each house and see the things happening there, you will be totally shocked. Women sit with matters and hold on to their marriages. With God by your side my sister, your marriage will survive and blossom. If that man was the right man for you right from the beginning, you will make it and find joy.

So what if he has cheated? This is the issue many women face and some men.

Men are less tolerant to the misdeeds of their wives, especially the ones involving another man, but women, many have forgiven their husbands for such, and more. At some point, the men grow up and grow out of it, but there are a few that go to their graves still cheating.

Well, you would not expect such from a born-again husband, right? Well you should not, but even in church, even pastors are known to be cheaters. For whatever reason, some men seem not to be satisfied with the one woman. Some women cheat as a retaliation to the cheating of their husband. Whatever the reason, it is sin, and it must not be done. If it has happened, let your heart forgive and move on.

It is too painful, you may say. Yes it is painful, but Jesus forgave those who nailed Him on the cross. Whilst He was still hanging on the cross with blood dripping from His hands and feet, His side and His head. He forgave them even though they never repented or even apologized. Only a centurion soldier confessed, *"Truly this Man was the Son of God."* Mark 15:39. Forgiveness is not a feeling but a choice you make even when the feelings tell you differently. Unforgiveness is a powerful force that will keep you down and in bondage as you can't move from what happened, going over the matter again and again. Learn to forgive.

In some instances divorce happens even against your wishes. Some men even have the nerve to sell the house and serve their wives with divorce papers without talking about it. Many women are kicked out of their homes by new owners because the husband has sold the house without telling the wife, a coward and a fool.

He will one day stand before God and answer why he did that to you and your children. Yours is to realize that such acts are not normal and are not of God.

Many women have stuck to their guns, the armor of God and prayed their marriages through. Some husbands have found their way home after many years of being lost. Such are powerful women that hold on to their vows and dare God to change their situation and bring their husbands back.

Allow me to say, you have the strength that your sister has. The same strength that made the other lady to pray through her marriage is also available for you. The same Spirit of God is available to strengthen you through it all.

Let God be the third Man in your marriage, as He was with the three Hebrew boys in the midst of a fire. He has not changed. He loves you with an everlasting love. He wants only the best for you. There is absolutely nothing good that He will withhold from you. He wants to give you His best, yours is to align yourself with His will. Let your decisions be comfortable and aligned with God. When there are still doubts, pray more until you find peace with the matter.

I have been married for more than a decade now. I know and can testify that marriage is not easy. I also know that my husband is definitely not my father, so I have learned not to compare them. I have also learned that men are not dogs as some ladies seem to think. I have also learned that men have their own mistakes just like I do.

I cannot say I have a perfect marriage, there is no perfect marriage. There is no such a thing as a perfect husband. I cannot be perfect, but I am being perfected until Christ comes and I put on the immortal and incorruptible. I therefore should not even put such an expectation on another human being.

I can safely say that, being married for so long, I am so used to this life that I don't see myself any other way.

My sister asked me, if I were to be given a chance to choose again, will I choose my husband. I said yes. I know the one I have, I would not want to start again learning about a new husband.

There are so many good things about him. If I looked at another man, I would find other things that could irritate me as well. No one is perfect.

Do not be afraid to love simply because someone else has had a bad experience. Let God lead you to your husband and pray earnestly. Let God give you a new perspective about men. Let your heart appreciate the differences we have.

You are of God, loved and cherished. Men are also of God loved and cherished. The both of you are God's idea of marriage between the church and Christ. Let this shadow be a good one for people to behold and anticipate, the love relationship with the Lord.

9

Let God heal you

When you look back in your life, there are people that have hurt you child of God. They have hurt you so badly that the wounds have not healed. You still remember their deeds and feel the anger aroused and you wish they would disappear before the face of the earth. You may wish God would just punish them and give them a taste of their own medicine. You may be feeling justified in the way you feel.

Some things happen in our lives for a purpose. You may not understand why it is happening, but God knows it and knows the end of a thing before it even begins. Some have blamed God for a lot of wrong things that have happened in their lives. At times we say it is the will of God that this thing should happen.

Think about Job for a while. This was a good man, blameless, there was no one like him at that time. God saw his life and noticed that this man was righteous. From the fall of man, the devil has been corrupting people and a few have been able to remain without sin. In fact, with God's standards, no man can stand and say they have no sin. Job always sought to please God and He was pleased.

Job saw that his children were partying too much and were prone to sinning during the parties.

Come to think of it, Job was not comfortable with the parties but he did not stop them. Instead, Job went to sacrifice to God to ask for forgiveness for his sons and daughters, just in case they had sinned during the party.

Meanwhile, there was a conversation in heaven between Satan and God. God asked if Satan had noticed Job, the man who feared the LORD and was blameless.

To Satan it was a contest to see if man can stand the test of temptation and testing. To God it was an affirmation that there are righteous people on the earth even where sin abounds. God knew that Job could withstand testing of his conduct. He allowed Satan to go ahead and test Job to see if he would change and sin against God.

When everything is going well, it is easier to live a life that pleases God. If something goes wrong, you begin to look for alternatives. Job was tested, he lost everything but still remained blameless. Satan went back to God and raised an issue that Job was still blameless because he had not been touched physically. God allowed Satan again to go back and test Job. Job was tested in his body, he was afflicted in a painful way. His wife even told him to curse God and die. It was way too much for a man to endure, but Job endured.

The end of this matter, was that Satan did not win. Job remained blameless before God. He remained trusting God through the troubles he went through. His faith did not fail him. I am raising this story because Job suffered a great deal. It would have been easier for Job to blame God, that He was not good because He did not protect him. It was easier to say God did that to him. The things that happened to Job were out of the ordinary. Some of his friends even blamed Job, saying that he must have sinned against God to be punished like that.

Job suffered serious pain, in his heart with the loss of his children and wealth. He suffered in his body with the sores he had. It was painful to lose everything at once, but he held on to God. He trusted God throughout his painful ordeal, and God came back and restored him. Job was healed completely and had other children, more beautiful. He had more wealth than he had before. The tears he shed were wiped away by the Lord.

God did not hurt Job, He allowed Job to be hurt by Satan. God had a plan to restore his loss right from the beginning. God knew that Job had the ability to endure it all. He would not have bragged about Job being blameless if he knew that he would not be able to remain faithful to God.

The time of restoration and joy was bound to come in Job's life, all he had to do was to endure and trust God.

Look at your own life. You will see that there are situations that have happened that you know you have not done anything to deserve such. You ask yourself why this is happening to you. You even begin to doubt the love of God. You think God does not love you simply because you are hurting. Well, Girl Child, God's love is not a yo-yo. His love does not bounce up and down because of circumstances. His love never changes even though you are going through stuff.

Look at things through the life of Job. He did nothing to deserve what happened to him but it still happened. He went through it all and came out of it a richer person. Think of the victory and joyful shout in heaven every time Satan lost the battle. Think of how proud God was when He saw that even through it all Job still remained blameless.

Don't let the circumstance you are facing now change your good character. Don't let other people's actions determine your response.

Decide to do right and be steadfast in doing right even when things are not going well for you.

In due season, God will restore you.

You may have also lost someone you love, a family member or a friend. You may think that God is not there simply because you have lost your loved ones. Well, Job, lost all his children and was still able to say, blessed be the name of the Lord.

It is God who is able to heal you in due course child of God. He only knows how deep your wound is. He knows what you need to come out of the situation you are facing. He is not necessarily pleased by the way things have turned out, but God has confidence in the ability He has deposited in you, that of endurance.

Don't look at yourself and think you will not survive. When you do that you are not trusting God's ability in you. Don't look at your own flesh to survive because it is temporary. Let the spirit rise within and be aligned with God and remain steadfast in your faith even through the season of difficulty.

Some people may think that being strong means they must not even cry. Just read the Psalms and you will realize just how David and the other psalmists cried out to the LORD. When you cry out to God, you are not weak, but you are refreshing yourself in God. You acknowledge that you need Him and that only He is able to take you through the situation at hand. Cry out to God, He is your Father and he is able to wipe the tears off your face and restore you.

Restoration may not always be to bring you back to the state you were. Job did not have his first children raised from the dead. He was restored as a parent, he had other children. His body was restored to perfect health.

He had wealth, even more than he had before.

Child of God, when God restores you, He knows what is best for you. Don't sit and wait for God to bring back exactly what you had before. You will remain miserable whilst waiting for what you had to come back. When you have lost a loved one, unless they are raised from the dead immediately, bury them and look forward to life without them. Don't sit and wait for God to bring back a loved one you lost years ago. This requires a reality check. There are things that once lost, cannot be regained, but you can open yourself up to receive something good from God. It may not be the same as before, but better.

You cannot sit and mourn for the rest of your life child of God, your husband is gone forever in this life time. Your child is gone forever in this life time. So is your mother and father, sister or brother or just whomever you have lost. In this life time, you have to accept that those who are gone will not come back. Live your life with the expectation of finding happiness even without the ones you loved. It can never be easy, but you cannot sit back and not move on with life as if the dead will come back.

Let God heal your wound, find your hope in God.

One of the downside of not healing after you have been hurt is that you may begin to hurt those around you. You may become bad company as you are constantly moaning about your loss. Even worse is if you have lost a relationship, the person you love walked out on you. Crying and remaining bitter will not make that man love you again.

Girl, hating him and whomever he has decided to move on with, is not going to make any difference in his life, but it will leave you bitter. You will live a miserable life whilst the other person is enjoying life. This calls for you to decide to take care of yourself, your heart and your life.

Dear Girl Child

The things Daddy's girls do to get back at those who have hurt them are horrible. There you are, beautifully and wonderfully made, running around with love potions so that a man who clearly does not deserve you, might be forced to love you, that's witchcraft child of God. You cannot make him love you. It can never be real love. Such things are temporary and reversible. Where will you be when he gets delivered from your love potion? Such things are not done, not by those made in the image of God.

Remember that when the time comes for you to stand before God, He will require an account from you, concerning your own actions. You cannot play the game of Adam saying, *"The woman whom You gave to be with me, she gave me of the tree and I ate."* Genesis 3:12. God has entrusted you with your own life, the actions of others He will require an account from them, not you.

Many women are in jail for killing their husbands, or the girlfriends of their husbands. The life and relationship they tried to preserve did not stand a chance of survival after imprisonment. Sadly, even in the house of God, these things happen.

Daughter of the Most High God, whenever you are hurt, there is only one who can heal you better than revenge. There is only one who will wipe your tears and leave you a better person. He has experienced pain and rejection, He has been hurt before. Jesus was betrayed by the one who ate in the same bowl with Him. The same one who held the money bag.

He was one of the chosen ones out of the whole nation. That was the one who sold Him for 30 pieces of silver.

Jesus knows how it feels to be betrayed. He is in a better position to tell you to receive your healing and go and enjoy life. When Jesus went through the courts, only a few disciples were there, Peter and possibly Matthew. The rest ran away and left Him to face prosecution alone. Jesus came back to the 11 disciples and still entrusted them with the gospel.

There is life after betrayal and hurt. There is life after loss, no matter how great is that loss. You cannot give up on life because of what you have lost. Let Jesus heal you so you can be a blessing to others.

There is probably at least one person out there who needs to hear your story and be encouraged to arise, even after a hurtful situation. God can use you to touch the lives of others, but you must be well first, so others can be helped through your testimony.

The woman with the issue of blood was healed first before the girl could be healed. The girl in fact died whilst Jesus was delayed attending to the woman with the issue of blood. Jesus healed the woman. The father of the girl was told to forget it because the child was dead, but Jesus went to raise her up.

If you don't have a scar to show, you are probably still a baby. My scars tell me that I have come out victorious. They tell me that the pain has passed, this is just a memory of what happened.

There are times when I remember what people have done to me. There are people that I wonder how I will react if I see them again.

At times, I think it would be better if they were dead, but, God has no victory in death, for the dead have no second chances. Going back again to what happened is like opening the scar tissue and watching blood come out and the pain starting all over again.

Dear Girl Child

I take comfort in the words of Jesus, *"Father, forgive them, for they do not know what they do."* Luke 23:34. Your healing starts at the point where you forgive those that hurt you.

I am also comforted in knowing that Jesus, having experienced physical pain to His body, and emotional pain, He knows how it feels to be hurt. He is in a better position to help me get through situations. There is no better High Priest than the one who experienced pain, so He can minister healing to us all.

Jesus is mindful of your hurt. He wants to heal you. Let Him heal you.

10

At the feet of Jesus

A story is told in the bible, about a sinful woman who found her place at the feet of Jesus. She had done all the wrong things in her lifetime, and had found like King Solomon that it was all vanity. Her temporary enjoyment was not fulfilling at all. She had probably made a living out of a life that she was not so proud of, but she survived. She was not proud of herself, but her day came, Luke 7:38-50.

This was a woman who was not liked in her community because of her conduct. People who saw themselves as holier than her looked down upon her. Yes, she was guilty of wrong doing many times, she had transgressed the Law of Moses many times, she had rendered herself unclean many times. She needed a lot of blood of bulls and whatever animals were required for the atonement of her sins.

Her community had probably used her as a teaching tool for their children. "Do not be like that girl from that corner house, she is no good." She was not the kind of person a guy would proudly bring to his parents' house as a bride. She was dirty in the eyes of men and through the law. She did not deserve to be in the company of holy and righteous people. Would she ever be forgiven?

One day, she saw Jesus, she heard about how good this Man was. She heard how He healed the sick, hugged the lepers, cast out devils, and opened the blind men's eyes.

Dear Girl Child

She heard how He healed first and released sinful people to go and sin no more. She heard that He set a new standard, not the law. He forgave sinners, they did not bring blood of animals to Him. He was a Rabbi, a teacher.

She saw Him at dinner, He was in the company of His disciples. These were the same men who told the blind men to stop making noise when they asked for mercy from Jesus. These were the same men who told the Master to tell the woman whose daughter was demon possessed to go away for she was also making a noise. His company was not as kind as this Man was to people.

She did not deserve to get into that house. She was too low class to be in the company of important people like those at the table. She was determined to go there and find herself a spot. She had a perfume, a very expensive one, she was not rich and that was probably the most expensive item she had. She had worked hard for it, though not in an honorable way. She took it, she was not going to buy her way into the dinner.

She wanted acceptance, she wanted forgiveness, she wanted compassion, she wanted love, and she wanted hope. She could not get it anywhere in the village as she was not worthy. She saw Him, she saw her spot, and she asked no permission from anyone, she went for Jesus. She knelt at His feet and poured her perfume on Him, she wiped His feet with her own hair. She had no towel, she had no bowl, and there was nothing fancy about what she was doing, except that she needed it more than Jesus did. He did not chase her away. He did not mind the expensive perfume. He did not mind even the stares from the people.

She was accepted, just as she was. There was nothing great that she could do to be accepted except to take herself to the Master and lay down her life before Him.

He knew stuff, even the hidden secrets. She didn't have to tell Him her lifelong sins. She just had to present herself at His feet and cry for mercy, love and compassion.

The owner of the house was offended. This was a sinful woman, who was not invited for dinner. She was sort of harassing the guest of honor, in today's language, but the guest of honor did not mind, in fact, He came for the very same sinful people. Jesus reprimanded him for he had not taken care of his guest as the woman did. He had not washed the feet of his guest, but this woman had done so. The dinner he provided was not from a repentant heart, but a proud self-righteous heart.

Jesus came for the sinners not the righteous.

The woman is not named in the scripture above. There is a story also told, of Mary the sister of Lazarus. She took an opportunity at the feet of Jesus. She anointed His feet with oil and wiped it with her hair. John 12:1-8.

One of the disciples was also offended, the perfume was expensive. She could have sold it at the market for a fortune and fed the poor. As if Judas cared for the poor. To him, money was more important than the gesture of that woman. However, to Jesus, the silver and the gold belongs to Him, the cattle on the thousand hills belongs to Him, the earth and its fullness belongs to Him, what can you offer Him that He does not own?

Have you not been in that situation Girl Child? If you have never sinned in your life, you still have the sin of Adam to which you and I are accused of. God has not developed a scale for small or big sins. Sin is sin, and is measured the same. He is holy, and we ought to be holy, that's His standard. There are things that you and I do that can leave you feeling worthless. It may seem that you just can't shake off such a thing, you go back to it over and over.

You may have shaken it off, but society still holds it against you.

There is a place, child of God that is safe for your heart to be laid bare. It is at the feet of Jesus that the world seems not to exist, it is just you and the Lord, loving each other. It is at the feet of Jesus that you put down the things you have, your transgressions lay them down and take His love and go back to your house filled with joy and peace.

He will not judge you, but He will love you. His heart will not pound within with words, 'guilty, guilty, and guilty'. He points to the blood, His own blood and all is made well and put to the past.

There are times of refreshing at the feet of Jesus. After all is said and done, He sits and waits to have the pleasure of your company.

Your problem daughter of the Most High God is not that you don't see where Jesus is. It is not that you don't want to go to the feet of Jesus. Your problem is that you look at things, and people, and they discourage you from going to Jesus.

You think that the likes of the owner of the house will look at you as unworthy to sit at the feet of Jesus. You let the opinions of people discourage you from sitting at the feet of Jesus. The self-righteous people make you feel worthless, that you stand no chance before Master Jesus. They think they are better people. You listen to them too much.

So what if you had abortions before? Do you think the blood of Jesus is not sufficient to wash your sins away? They know you aborted, so what? They know you slept with that man and the other, then what?

There are many like that in church.

They will spread the story of your life to whomever cares to listen. They will judge you and find you unworthy even to talk to the pastor. They will not even consider that you have received Christ and your sins are forgiven. They will not consider to at least give you a chance to be build up by Jesus.

Jesus showed us that He is sufficient, all by Himself. You don't need the blood of bulls and goats before you can go to Jesus. You just need to get yourself there, the rest will be forgotten.

At times, you are your own worst enemy child of God. You look down on yourself. You remind yourself of your weaknesses too often and forget that in your weakness, His power is strengthened. You let low self-esteem prevent you from taking your position at the feet of Jesus.

Come, take the step, and go for Jesus. He waits for you to come and lay down all to Him, give Him the right to mess you up before He fixes you up. Allow Jesus to turn your life upside down and rebuild it again. Come to a place where your tears matters. With no tissues or towels, this woman used herself to wipe the feet of the Master. All you need is in you, Jesus wants your whole self to make you a new and better person.

You cannot wash yourself and then go to Jesus. You cannot change yourself and then go to Jesus. What will be the point of sending Jesus to die for us if we were all sufficient by our own self? The truth is, you and I need Jesus.

That woman needed the love and compassion of Jesus more than Jesus needed His feet to be washed. Jesus' feet could have been washed by anyone, even the owner of the house anytime.

Jesus could have washed His feet as He normally did daily, but that woman would have remained with her own fears, rejection, guilt and all, if she did not go down on her knees to wash the feet of the Master. She needed to be accepted by God Himself and then society would realize that they had entered a season of grace. The law would have found many things through which they could find her guilty. She was no saint, she was a sinner.

Just like the woman caught in adultery. She was brought to Jesus and there she found grace on two feet. She was guilty, and the people made sure everyone knew that. Though she did not take herself to Jesus, she nevertheless found the same grace. Jesus knelt down and started writing whilst the people persecuted Him, they wanted an answer. Would He implement the Law of Moses or would He show grace?

At the feet of Jesus, this woman was given a second chance, she was told to go and sin no more. She was ushered into a new era, of grace, of forgiveness of sins, of mercy and the love of God. Her secret was out in the open, she had nothing more to lose. She was exposed, but she was forgiven. She would start again and do the right things and leave her sinful nature behind.

Martha and Mary had different experiences. Martha was very busy, too busy to sit at the feet of Jesus. She was mindful of the things of the flesh. She was busy cooking, preparing food for the guests, but as Jesus said, His meat was to do the will of God. Mary had chosen the best thing. She chose to sit at the feet of Jesus. She would not lose out on the wisdom of the Master.

The Lord would rather have a conversation with you at His feet than you busy taking care of His needs.

There are times when you have to leave everything and sit and listen to what the Lord is saying to you, when He speaks, sit down and listen.

Another woman who knew the importance of being at the feet of Jesus was the woman whose daughter was demon possessed, Mark 7:24-30. She had a problem that she could not resolve by herself. She found the one Man who could help her. He was busy with His disciples, but she did not consider that. She fell at His feet and worshiped the Lord to help her daughter. Jesus did not answer at first and the disciples were annoyed. They asked Him to send her away.

When Jesus eventually replied, He told her that it was not good that He takes the bread from the children and give it to the dogs. She did not qualify to get a thing from Jesus. She was likened to a dog. Another person would have left disappointed because of these words. She had heard good things about this Jesus, but there she was being told she did not qualify.

This woman, at the feet of Jesus, would not let Him go. When you fall at the feet of someone, you are actually blocking their way. You are commanding their attention. You are saying, they cannot not go anywhere until they have attended to you. She did not want special treatment, she wanted something, anything, and as long as it came from Jesus it was sufficient. She did not want the whole meal, the crumbs were sufficient for her.

At the feet of Jesus, she took what she was given. She was determined not to go back without her breakthrough. She was not going to let Him go. She wanted His attention and she got it. She worshiped Him, she showed Jesus that He was her only hope. She did not have a plan B, Jesus alone was sufficient for her.

That is a very powerful position to take.

Your situation will be dealt with if you took your time and go down on your knees and worship the Lord your God. Surrender it all to Jesus, sit there until He gives you your request. Sit there even when others tell you that you are a nuisance. Sit there even when you feel like Jesus has no intention of granting you your request. Sit there, until He gives you attention.

Don't let people discourage you from getting what you desire from the Lord.

Do you trust Jesus enough to wait for Him? She pestered Him to the point where He gave her attention. His silence did not mean He did not hear her. She did not put a request in a prayer box and left. She did not send a message to request for help. She did not ask someone to ask on her behalf. She went there by herself and sat there for her daughter's healing.

Don't give up too easily child of God. Don't move away simply because you think your answer is taking too long. Don't listen to people telling you that you are wasting your time with your prayer request. Don't listen to voices telling you that you don't deserve this. You Father has already told you that He will grant you the desires of your heart. He knows what your needs are, He expects you to hold on to Him until it is time for Him to give it to you.

I remember a time when I used to cry for my children. This was a time for me to sit at the feet of Jesus until He gave me attention. This was a time where I depended on Him only for I would not be able to live without my children.

One time I was so angry, disappointed and hurt that I kneeled down next to my bed, banging the bed and the floor. I remember saying that Jesus must come down now and tell me what was going on here.

I was fresh from church and an incident happened that made me wonder why I was at church in the first place if God would not watch over my children.

I was dealing with rebellious teenagers and it was as if God was not even bothered. I learned over time that God is mindful of me and He is taking care of my situations even when it does not seem like He is. At His feet, I gave it all to Him. He did not grace my room, but was already within me. He held me up to stand and remain standing. I would not let my children go to the enemy, God would not let them go either.

When you kneel down, the person who is standing is superior to you. You are subservient to that person.

You may be an important person somewhere else, when you kneel, you acknowledge that there is someone superior to you. Jesus has power to deal with your situation. At His feet you acknowledge that He is more powerful and that you depend on Him.

Don't leave the feet of Jesus until He has given you what you have requested. Like Jacob, wrestle until He blesses you.

11

You are okay

What is it child of God that makes you think others are better than you? What makes you think you have to put on make-up and pretend to be beautiful before you can be seen in public? You put on a persona, an act because you think people will not take you as you are.

God's beloved daughter, you are a fine person, you are okay in the eyes of God. You are not as bad as you think. God sees the positive things in you, He sees potential, and He sees victory. God knows he has put His strength in you. He knows that you can pull through that situation. He knows you are more than a conqueror even when you don't think so.

With all the weaknesses, the stumbling and falling you have gone through, the Lord still accepts you. The Lord still wants to use you. Whatever it is that makes you seem like you do not qualify to be used by God, remember, He causes all things to work together for the good of those who love Him.

Remember, God is a Potter and you are clay in His hands. When you look at clay, shapeless and ugly, you will not see the beautiful vase that will come out of the clay once the Potter is done. The clay is okay in the eyes of the Potter, shapeless as it is, it is just okay. The Potter sees the vase, the idea is clear, the plan and design is clear. The Potter knows even where the vase will be used once finished. He does not mind how the clay looks now, He can shape it.

If you spend too much of your time feeling useless, you will not see the potential in who you are to become the beautiful vase.

What has been talked about in the preceding chapters is just like the process of spinning the clay which begins to shape into a vase. It is at that point that things are put in the right place, the excess clay is thrown away. The clay spins uncontrollably, at high speed until it shapes up nicely. If you were to stop the vase making process halfway, you will have an ugly, shapeless object that you cannot use. If the clay could talk, it will tell you that it is not easy to spin like that.

This is the process of pruning in your life that shapes you to become who God wants you to be. He says He is the vine dresser, He prunes the vine so it will bear much fruit. He removes the things that stand in the way of the fruitfulness of the vine so it can reach its full potential. He shapes the vine so it looks good as well, but the pruning is not an easy process.

The vine dresser does not cut off the whole vine simply because it does not look good. No, He looks at the vine with the eyes that see potential. He sees that once He has cut this and that little branch, the vine will look beautiful, and bear much fruit. He cuts out the corners, the things protruding out of the vine in an ugly way, those have to go.

God has great and wonderful plans for our lives. He knows what is best for us even though we do not see it. We may not see the potential beautiful vase that will come out of the spinning process, but God sees it and He likes the end-product. God does not discard the clay or the vine that looks ugly, He takes it as it is and makes it what He wants.

Your problem child of God is that you want to shape yourself, make yourself ready for God to use you, and you always fall short. You try to fix this and that about you instead of submitting to God to fix you. When you come to Him looking shapeless as you are, He will make a beautiful vase out of you.

God has used people that did not fit the bill before, and He made them great people. King Saul was not kingly material. He had a very bad low self-esteem, he did not think he could be used by God to lead the people, but God took him and made him a warrior.

However, although God had pruned Saul and he became a mighty warrior and won many battles, when the things God had pruned began to grow again, Saul did not submit to God to prune him again. He lost it because He would not obey God, but it shows that though he did not see himself as qualifying for God's assignment, he was still God's choice for that time.

A great example of pruning is in the story of Gideon. Although in this case it was not a direct pruning to Gideon. God wanted to remove the excess people so that the few remaining would be fruitful. From 32000 soldiers, ready for war, God required that they be reduced. The number was reduced to 22000 and it was still too much for God to use. Eventually, there were only 300 men remaining to go to war. This was a small number compared to the enemy, whose soldiers were as numerous as the sand in the seashore.

God removed what was not required in the army. Gideon had brought the whole army and made it subject to the plan of God. It was God who decided what the team would look like for that specific battle.

At times before, more soldiers would have been required, but this time, it was God who decided that they ought to be less.

On your own beloved daughter, you will not know how much of what you need in your life, but if you give yourself to God, He will remove what is not required, so that you become more fruitful. Sometimes you think you need your friends in order to succeed in life. You think you need connections to make it in life. You think on your own with God you are not sufficient, if you, however, sit and begin to scrutinize yourself and decide what you think is right or wrong in your life without God, you run short. Only God has a better view.

Imagine if Gideon did not consult with the Lord, he would have used the whole army, and that strategy was not the best for that battle. It is God who knows what the best for each battle is. You come to Him as you are and He will make in you an army ready for battle.

The more you sit and scrutinize yourself, the more frustrated you become. For you see that you are not sufficient in a certain area and you have no solution for it. You alone entertain the devil who will tell you that you will not succeed. You will entertain thoughts that say don't even try. You will entertain thoughts that says this is not for people like you so don't even try. However when you come to God as you are, He will tell you if it is okay for you, He will prepare you and make you ready for it.

So girl, you are okay for that job. When you walk with God, He will tell However, which of the jobs is best for you. When you go by yourself, you will take up any job and be miserable.

When you do not consult God, you will at times refuse jobs because you don't think you qualify, but when you are aligned with God, He prepares you for the job, He finds it for you and takes you through the application process.

When Jesus chose the 12 disciples, He did no wait for them to be perfect first. In fact, they never became perfect at all. He chose the uneducated and low state people. He did not go to the Pharisees and Sadducees who thought they were educated in the law. They would have been too difficult to use because they would have argued the law all the time.

Peter was impulsive, abrasive, fearful, and proud and so on, but Jesus took him as he was and pruned him. Peter had to fail many times so he could learn and be sharpened. He was first to answer and still got it wrong, embarrassing himself and Jesus, but Jesus took that as an opportunity to teach him, and such lessons were good for the establishment of the church.

When Jesus told them about His impending death, Peter arose in His defense to a point where Jesus said, *"Get behind Me, Satan!"* Matthew 16:23. It was probably the most painful words Peter heard from Jesus directed at him. Peter had to learn to look at things in the eyes of God, not looking at gratifying the flesh.

Think about it, the death of Jesus was not a desirable thing for the disciples. They had grown to love their Master, they had seen great miracles and were sure that He was the Messiah.

It was natural for Peter to react that way, just as he cut the ear of the servant when they were in the garden before Jesus was arrested. It was in the character of Peter to try and resolve an issue. Jesus wanted that character in Peter exposed so He can prune it and make a grounded, solid leader of the church.

If Peter were to try to change himself, it would not work.

He would not know what needs to be changed in him. He had three years with Jesus, but even till the end, he still did not understand that it was God's will that Jesus should die for the sins of many. He still wanted to resolve the issue himself.

When the Holy Spirit was poured out, Peter was ready to serve the Master and build the church. He had gone through the pruning process. He was okay when he came to Jesus, He wanted him like that so He could make a disciple, an apostle and leader of the church out of him. Jesus knew what had to be removed from Peter. He had nothing to be ashamed about. He was okay for Jesus, He could work with that.

Many are called by the Lord for His service. You sit around and refuse to serve God because you check yourself, you assess yourself and find that you are not worthy for the call of God. Who is? You scrutinize yourself and find many shameful sins and then conclude that Jesus wants the perfect and pure people to use them for ministry. You assess yourself and find that you don't know the word so well so you cannot preach the gospel.

You allow people to tell you their opinion about who qualifies to serve God and in what position. They tell you what is best for you when they don't even know you. They tell you not to do certain things because they have assessed you and found you fall short, but wait child of God, all these people and even you are not the Potter. You do not know how to make a beautiful vase, you need to submit to the Potter so He can decide what kind of vase He wants to make out of you.

Your design is already in the hands of the Potter. Whatever shape you make out of your own thinking will never be the same as what the Potter has designed. You will keep trying and fail to make yourself look good.

Submit yourself to the Potter, allow Him to spin you a while and shape you. Allow Him to take the excess clay and throw it away. Allow Him to put beautiful color and make you bright.

When the Potter is done, the vase will be ready to be used by the Master. You will lack nothing and will look good in what you do for the Lord. Look around you, there are people who looked terrible when they got saved. They were in a bad state. Some took months to be delivered and set free from demonic possession and oppression, but once that was done, they looked and behaved differently. You too can change, but come to God as you are.

No one goes to the bathroom to bath after they had a bath. Do not think Jesus wants you to come to Him after you have cleaned up your act, no, He wants you in the state where you don't even like yourself much. He said come to me all you who are heavy laden, and I will give you rest, not those who are free. When you think you are too bad for Jesus, it is the right time to go to Him.

He is not judgmental, He knows our mistakes. He knows we are dust born into a sinful nature that is weak and prone to make mistakes. He knows we try our best, but our best is not good enough. He then says, try me, then your best will come out. You may try by yourself, but unless the Lord builds a house, he who builds it labors in vain. So stop your effort and submit to God.

This is a time where you see yourself and tell Jesus to fix you up. This is where you don't hide your faults like the cellulite hidden with tights, right ladies?

This is where you allow Jesus to take you on a journey of self-discovery, restoration, renewal and growth. You cannot be left behind because you are still covering yourself up with make-up. Leave the make-up, let the tears fall down, let them mess you up and sit whilst Jesus wipes them off.

You are not a difficult project for Jesus, He has dealt with more difficult characters. If He can shape Peter, you are not so bad. What about Paul? You are not so bad. How about Mary, from whom seven demons were cast out?

How about the woman at the well, after all the five husbands and the sixth one, Jesus still saw the potential in her. He spoke to the one to whom He was not even supposed to be seen with in the same place. He asked for water from she whom He was not supposed to share a cup with. He spent some time with a woman of unacceptable character. He used her to get into Samaria and preach the gospel.

The community came in numbers and said *"Now we believe, not because of what you said, for we ourselves have heard Him and we know that this is indeed the Christ, the Savior of the world."* John 4:42.

The people might have misjudged her all along. No one knows why she had 5 husbands before. Jesus did not say she had 5 boyfriends, He said husbands, but the 6th one was not hers. So, there was just something not right with this woman, but Jesus used her to penetrate Samaria. People even forgot about her hideous past and embraced the news she was bringing.

I am a quiet person naturally. I speak less and listen more. Some think I am boring, but I like my quiet times. Jesus saw it fit to use me to minister to others. You can believe that I am quiet, but let's start a discussion about Jesus, we can go to the United Kingdom and back with me talking.

A dear friend experienced that one time, we flew to Wales talking all the way and back. She told people we met back home, 'this woman talks a lot'.

On my own, I would not have known the potential to talk a lot was in me, but Jesus, knowing He needed someone to talk, He chose the very quiet person for the job. Talk about 'bad choice'. The other deficiency I have is that I don't like writing. I thank God for the computers, bless those who invented it. If I were to write by hand, I would not finish, but today, I am a writer, typist, so to say. I never thought I would write books, but I have. I spoke it once prophetically and it has happened.

If ministering was for the holy ones, I would not qualify. My sins are too many to count. If you think yours are better than mine, then we will have a meaningless discussion. The bottom line is this, God chooses, qualifies and sends out.

You may sit and debate whether you qualify to be called all your lifetime. You will at some point accept it, but you will miss out on the great work you would have done if you accepted earlier. God has entrusted you with great works, you just have to step off yourself and step into God.

People are waiting for you, child of God to arise and shake off all those shackles and go for victory. Someone might not meet Christ until you get to Christ first. Someone might not be healed until you are healed. Someone might remain depressed because you have not come out of your own self issues. You are a solution awaiting to be unveiled. Look around you, someone needs help whilst you are sitting and looking down at yourself because of some mistakes and shortcomings.

Come running, come walking, come jumping, and crawl if you must but come, Jesus awaits.

12

A mighty girl's army

The generation of women that raised us came from a time in history where girls had a distinct place, in the kitchen, barefoot and pregnant. A generation arose that went beyond teaching and nursing professions to taking the boardrooms as Chairpersons and CEOs.

The world awaits an army, a mighty army of girls and women. An army that will take over and bring order. The church has sheltered and brooded over this army, let the daughters of the Most High God be positioned for glory.

Ezekiel saw a phenomena in the valley of dry bones. He was led to the valley by the Spirit of the Lord and what he saw was not such a good sight. He saw bones, not just a few bones, but a lot of bones. They were very dry, there was no life in them. They had been dead a long time.

There is no hope to raise dead bones except for the awaited time of the return of Christ, but Ezekiel saw it, whilst we wait for it. These bones were in an open field, where everyone could see that they were indeed dry. Everyone did not expect that they could live.

The Lord asked Ezekiel, *"Son of man, can these bones live?"* Ezekiel 37:3. That was a strange question for Ezekiel. He had never seen dead bones coming to life, but, he also knew that he was with the author of life, who brings to life what does not exist. Out of nothing, He creates and life begins.

For Ezekiel, the Creator knew better. The society he lived in had only one understanding, those bones were dead, period, but the one who made the bones was asking him a question that did not make sense, but still, there must have been a good reason why the Lord would ask such a question. A little hope, a possibility!

So, Ezekiel replied, *"Oh Lord God, You know"*. Ezekiel 37:3. He was not prepared to answer things he did not know of, lest he spoke outside of faith. He did not know, he had never heard of such a thing happening anywhere.

The one thing that stood between life and those bones was the instruction the Lord gave to Ezekiel – *"Prophesy to these bones, and say to them, 'O dry bones, hear the word of the LORD! Thus says the Lord God to these bones: "Surely I will cause breath to enter into you and bring flesh upon you, cover you with skin and put breath in you; and you shall live. Then you shall know that I am the LORD."* Ezekiel 37:4-6.

The bones would have remained dead if Ezekiel did not step in to speak to them words of life. They would have remained dead if he did not hear the word of the Lord and acted upon it. They needed a willing vessel to be used to bring them to life.

You see child of God, you have the authority on earth over creation. Creation awaits the manifestation of the sons of God. Creation awaits redemption also. The trees awaits to hear the voice speaking to them.

The bones that were dead had no hearing but they heard the voice of Ezekiel. They rose, bone to bone, a rattling sound and they connected. Ezekiel spoke and breath came upon the bones and they came to life.

Arise child of God and speak life to dead bones.

Arise and do the miraculous, in your area of influence for the glory of God. You were born for such a time as this.

Be it at school young lady, take your position. Don't sit and fret over dead things, speak life. Don't sit and look over problems, they will never change until and unless you speak to them.

Unless you hear the voice of God and move in to do as instructed, there will be no change in your life.

Someone has to solve that problem in your area. Every new design, every innovation comes because someone saw a problem and did not sit around wishing it away, they came up with a solution. Some solutions may require trial and error until you get it right. The bones did not live at the first prophetic word, Ezekiel had to speak again and change tactic. They had connected, but did not breathe. They needed breath, and he prophesied breath and there was life.

Therefore child of God, do not be discouraged when you speak to the bones and they don't respond first time around by coming alive. When you take the instructions of the Lord and do as He says, they will hear you and live.

This is an army of girls in the various areas in society that must rise and bring life. Parliament needs politicians that have a backbone and can stand up for the community at large. You can arise and go prophecy life to parliament for the glory of God.

Why should CEOs of big conglomerates be male dominated still? Girls are studying, getting degrees, being innovative. Will the army of girl CEOs arise and take up their positions? When Ezekiel speaks, the army must respond and come alive.

Churches have seen a rising of female ministers of the Gospel even under difficult positions. We have already addressed how we should support each other as women. Previous chapters have already addressed the issue of pulling each other down.

The type of Mary and Elizabeth, Naomi and Ruth are required here. Daughters of God need to arise and occupy until Jesus comes. Wherever God places you, you need to occupy it. People must know that they can come to you for assistance.

Let there be a recognition of the great role played by women. Historically, and biblically, the work of women did not take center stage. However, even with the little attention they got, there are still great records in history. You too girl have a role to play in the records of history.

History is made in the present and told in the future. What will the generations to come learn from our generation? Will your name be found written about the great works you did? Jesus has gone to the Father, it is time for the greater works (John 14:12).

The oil magnate

Out of a difficult situation, arose a oil magnate. She was a widow and the record of history tells us she was a troubled one. She had sons and their father had left a mess instead of a fortune. Someone had to pick up the pieces, fix them.

Her only sons were to be sold as slaves to pay the debt of her husband. Some women have faced that already, the debts your husband leaves behind throwing you into the deep end. She did not cause the situation but she was in it and had to fix it.

She had two choices, she could sit back and see her sons

taken away and be remembered as the widow who lost her sons to the loan sharks. Her second choice was that she would be remembered as the woman who arose and saved her sons.

She had no education or profession, she was a housewife. She had not known the finances of the house but she had to be in charge and start by fixing a mess. She did not even have a business idea that could help her out. Their debt was probably too much to warrant that two sons be taken as slaves.

This was a predicament that some women would just throw their hands in the air and cry for years on end, but not this woman. She was a woman of a different character. She did not have a solution but she knew one thing, her husband served God.

She went to the place where she knew God would show up. Her husband was one of the sons of the prophets. She found Elisha the prophet and told him the story. *"So Elisha said to her, "What shall I do for you? Tell me, what do you have in the house." 2 Kings 4:2.*

So, after telling the prophet her problem, the prophet pointed the solution back to her.

What she wanted was dependent on what she had. She came to the prophet having the solution in her house but she did not know it. Do you realize that you have a solution to your problems and that of the community? You are not just a poor and troubled widow, you have a solution right inside your house.

She answered, *"Your maidservant has nothing in the house but a jar of oil." 2 Kings 4:2.* She looked at the jar of oil as nothing significant.

However, she still remembered to state it though, she had nothing but a little oil. It was there but little, what could she do with such a little oil. She was in the presence of the servant of the Most High God.

She had stated her case and the solution was with her. Elisha told her to go borrow vessels from everywhere, empty vessels. Importantly, Elisha said, "Do not gather just a few". So, there had to be a famine of oil in the place and its surroundings for this woman's issue to be resolved. Why would the community keep empty vessels unless there was a challenge, no oil!

The poor and troubled widow became a solution to herself and the community. She went as instructed and collected many empty jars and went to her house. Elisha said, *"You shall shut the door behind you and your sons; then pour it into all those vessels, and set aside the full ones."* 2 Kings 4:4.

She had an instant business, she had to incubate it, behind closed doors. People would have come to see the phenomena if she worked outside, but God had revealed this to her, she had to keep it to herself. Let the people wonder where she got so much oil, but she would know.

She went in and started pouring her little oil, vessel after vessel, she poured. They were filled until there was no more vessel left in the house and the village. She went out and sold the oil to the very same people from whom she borrowed the vessels. She made enough money to pay her debt and more to live by.

She became an oil magnate, she became the solution to the need for oil in the village. Look around you Girl Child, what is challenging you and the society? You are a solution waiting to happen.

Until you rise up to enquire of the Lord, the problem remains unresolved. Your debts will continue to pile up. The country will remain with the challenge in the area where you are having a solution. Be innovative, be a problem solver, ask God, He will show you how.

The Lodge owner

When God calls His servants, He makes provision for them through the people on this earth. He does not rain down manna like He did in the time Israel was in the wilderness. In times past, a woman of Shunem took the responsibility for feeding Prophet Elisha every time he passed by their place. After doing this for some time, she decided on something a little more permanent.

"And she said to her husband, 'Look now, I know that this is a holy man of God, who passes by us regularly. Please, let us make a small upper room on the wall; and let us put a bed for him there, and a table and chair and a lampstand; so it will be, whenever he comes to us, he can turn in there." 2 Kings 4:9-10.

This Shunamite saw a gap in the life of the servant of God. Instead of him asking for lodging and food whenever he came around, she and her husband made a room for him upstairs. It was not just a room, it was a comfortable one with all the necessities. She did not call the village to show them what she did, she did not require permission except from her husband. She saw no need to declare this in the congregation for everyone to clap hands for her and bless her.

What she did in her private home was known by God and touched the heart of the servant of God to the point where he asked; *"What can I do for you?"* 2 Kings 4:13. Her efforts were realized, she did not have to ask anything. She did not ask anything. She replied, *"I dwell among my own people."* 2 Kings 4:13.

She was content with dwelling among her own people, with her husband, she did not see a reason to complain about anything. She was grateful. Israel had been through difficulties, so for her it was fine to be amongst her own people.

The one thing she did not have, a son. Elisha was told of this, and he said to her *"About this time next year you shall embrace a son."* 2 Kings 4:15. He did not lay hands on her, he did not cast out a demon of barrenness, he spoke a word and God fulfilled it the following year.

She had a son and continued with life gratefully. She had obtained the most precious gift that surpasses all the money she spent on Elisha. One time her son died and Elisha was not there. She went to find him, she told no one that the child had died. She knew that the prophet had caused her to have joy by a word, she had to get back her son through the same word from the prophet.

Gehazi came towards her, as she approached, he tried to push her away from the man of God. Elisha allowed her closer, she did not ask him to raise her son. She asked him *"Did I ask a son of my lord? Did I not say, 'Do not deceive me'?"* 2 Kings 4:28. She indeed had not asked for a son. She got it because the man of God had been grateful and wanted to bless her for the hospitality she had shown him.

Elisha went and raised her son, for the woman said to him, *"As the LORD lives, and as your soul lives, I will not leave you."* 2 Kings 4:30. She did not want anyone else to sort this out, but the man who started it in the first place. She was now determined to hold on to what God had given her, she could not let her son go.

There is so much negativity these days concerning giving, in the body of Christ, especially to a servant of God. Unfortunately, because of the misdeeds of a few people, our generation loses out on the benefits of daring God to bless us.

Also, the motive for giving has changed, from being kind to a servant of God to wanting recognition.

God searches the heart, knows the motive and knows how the matter will end up. He does not receive glory when you take it, child of God. He does not release a blessing for you to take the glory. He releases the blessing to an unpretentious and humble heart. You have nothing to boast about when you get blessed by God, you give glory to God.

Take an opportunity to look around at what you can do for God. When you do it, do it as unto the Lord and not as unto men. God will surely release even more blessings. Remember, this woman was giving because she was already blessed. She recognized that what she had, came from God already, and she released it to God who gave her what her money could not buy.

Your blessing may not come in a car, or a house, or a job, but it may be the greatest desire that no money can buy. What is it that you put as a memorial to God? Not that the blessings of God can be bought, but a memorial to God is appreciated, and provokes action.

As girls we at times have tendencies of wanting to be seen by people. Will you give your best pair of shoes to someone and not tell anyone at all? At times it is as if you want validation for the gift you have given over and above the recognition. Someone must clap hands that you have done a great thing.

The worst kind is the girlfriend who does something good for you so that others will feel pity for you. 'She is so poor, I gave her my old pair of shoes'. The next time you see someone in need, don't look around to see who is there to clap hands for you, give something and move on with life.

Your gift will find you in your hour of need.

God knows your need even before you tell Him. Could it be that you have not received your 'son' because you have not released your gift to whomever God sent you to give to? Don't wait till your 'husband' is old, give now, act now and see your gifts speaking on your behalf to your Father in heaven. You give because you have already been given, and your gifts will come as a memorial like they did with Dorcas in the book of Acts 9:36-40.

The Shunamite woman and Dorcas laid their treasures in heaven and they were remembered. It is your turn, child of God, to lay your treasures in heaven, you shall be remembered too.

The ruler

In this male dominated world of business, corporate and the church, you would be sure to get one or two people who tell you in this day and age that you can't do this because you are a woman. Remember this Girl Child, when God blessed the first people on earth, He blessed them male and female. He did not bless the male first and then the female later, but both.

Such stereotypes have set the daughters of God back by decades. Girls are still lagging behind trying to step up and run the race that men are running. You see child of God, it is not about competing with men for positions, but taking up positions because you are called by God for that position. It is because God has deposited what is needed in that position for that period.

When you chase after what men have you miss out on getting what God has prepared for you. It may be that you are chasing after a position which God has not prepared for you, whereas your position is even greater than the one you are chasing.

The woman Deborah, she was so comfortable in her calling. She had her priorities straight, God first, husband second. *"Now Deborah, a prophetess, the wife of Lapidoth, was judging Israel at that time."* Judges 4:4.

She was not threatened by the males around her. She did not mind that she was at the helm of Israel who was in trouble. She was the answer for Israel at that point in time. She did not possess physical strength like the men of war. She had a position and she occupied that position without being apologetic about it.

When the time to go to war came, she sent the soldiers. Barak refused to go without Deborah. He did not refuse because Deborah had more strength than him, but because she was in charge. Kings used to go to war with their soldiers. She was not one to sit down and look beautiful at the helm of Israel. She had to go out there and be there.

Deborah, recognizing that this man was not prepared to take his position to defeat the enemy, told him that the battle would be won through a woman. The soldiers would fight, but the one to destroy Sisera was the woman called Jael.

She gave direction, she operated in an unusual space. You can imagine having a woman President in South Africa who is also the head of the church. That's the space of Deborah, yet she was also the wife of a man.

God is expecting an army of women like Deborah who will enter the corridors of big corporations and yet still lead the church and be responsible wives to their husbands. Women who will not be afraid to exercise their authority over the people.

Now, this argument that a woman must not lead men must be put to rest at some point. It is still being used by people who are lazy to read the word of God. Such people cannot explain why someone else's wife was a Prophetess (Church Leader), a Judge (Country leader) and a wife (Submissive to her husband).

Let this argument rest here now and let people go and read why Paul said what he said to the women in that church.

The teacher

Having dealt with the subject of women ministers above, another woman of note was Priscilla. A Jewish woman in the era of Paul whose writing is used to pull women down from the pulpit was used of the Lord.

She and her husband Aquila came back from Rome and went to Ephesus together with Paul who then left them there. Another man called Apollos was there who knew the gospel of John and taught it diligently. This man needed to get the new gospel understanding so that he could preach.

In Acts 18:26 the Bible states, *"So he began to speak boldly in the synagogue. When Aquila and Priscilla heard him, they took him aside and explained to him the way of God more accurately."* This was a married couple that ministered together the gospel to this man.

The Bible does not say Aquila took Apollos aside, it says "they". It also does not say Priscilla did that alone, but that they worked as a team. They were not competing for a position of who knows the gospel better than the other. They wanted Apollos to continue ministering the true gospel.

It is also stated that they took him aside, meaning they did not embarrass him in front of the people. They had the unity of the body of Christ in mind in the way they ministered to him. He was a noted minister who they had to give respect and guide accordingly.

Now, if you think daughter of God that you are unable to minister because your husband is a minister, think again. If God has called you to minister alongside your husband, it does not make you a competitor but a fellow minister. Do not be intimidated by the role of your husband and do not get into arguments that compare you with your husband. Rather pray for the unity in ministering and fellowship that this couple displayed.

When you are required to stand for the truth of the gospel, you ought to do it as unto the Lord. You cannot back down when it comes to addressing other men simply because you are a woman. Let out what God has deposited in you.

Mainly, you are not a second-class citizen in the kingdom of God. You are not the last or the one at the bottom. Stand alongside your husband and minister the word of God.

Daughters today

What will history say about you daughters of the Most High God? Can the records keep what you have done in business, in ministry, in corporate, in politics? Will your name be written in tablets for generations to come?

Women in past generations innovated things like, the microwave, dishwasher, windshield wipers, closed circuit television and more.

The women of old did not have stronger characters than you, but they were just human. Their failures are recorded just as the grace of God propelled them to do greater things.

The kingdom of God has to expand and you and I have a role to play in it. Our place is not to compete but achieve. Ours is not a battle to trample on others to get to the top, but to realize that an army is never formed by one or just a few.

Dear Girl Child

The landscape can never be changed by one woman, or just the few. An army must arise and make an impact in this world.

As I conclude;

Would you place your mark in history?

Come now, child of God, you can do it;

The Lord is with you;

You are blessed beyond your imagination;

You are loved by your Father;

You are special to God;

You are here for a great purpose;

Grace and peace be upon you.

13

You are your Daddy's princess

Bonus Chapter by Nomsa Mashele

You have read the book to this point, congratulations! I believe the Lord has spoken to you and ministered to you to a point where you are comfortable in who you are in Him. This last chapter is a result of a discussion which I believe was inspired by the Lord between me and the author of this book. It was one of those 'got to meet this person' kind of meetings we had, me and my friend Carol.

My name is Nomsa, I am Daddy's Favored Princess. I am sharing a part of my life with you in this chapter because I have felt the love of my Father and would like you to share the same and even more. This chapter seeks to assure you even further that, precious daughter, you are your Daddy's princess.

Your Daddy is the King and you are His daughter. I am sure you know that being a princess is something you are born into. The day you accepted the Lord Jesus Christ as your Lord and Savior you were born again, and that gave you the right to be His princess. It is something that you inherit, and there should not be a struggle about it. However there are times when it becomes a struggle as you will see when I continue with my story.

A princess is special, is treated in a special way. A princess is loved and adored by her Father.

Dear Girl Child

She knows how special she is and she conducts herself in that way.

A princess just has to ask her Daddy and she is provided for, she is special and she knows that.

For me, seeing myself as Daddy's princess was something that didn't come naturally, it took me a long time to truly believe and live like His princess. I was born again on the 1st December 1998 but for me to start seeing myself as the princess that I am, it happened around 2011 and I must say that since then it has been a journey. There were days when I was confident in this truth that I am His princess and there are days that I found it hard to believe that I am His princess.

Ever present Father

For me, the journey has been a challenging one because I was raised by my mom, I got to see my dad about twice or so a month before their divorce and after the divorce I really go to see him I guess once a year or so. My mom was from Gauteng, she came to Mpumalanga because of her marriage to my dad. My dad however continued working in Gauteng and visited us every fortnight whilst we were growing up. For as long as I can remember we never had a full month with my dad at home, so I would only see him during the times that he came to visit us. Even though he did not stay with us full time, I have memories of family outings that we had, and they were fun moments even though they were few.

As a born again child of God, I had to come to the realization of the truth that my Father is there for me all the time. He is within me. He is not coming once every two weeks in a month or once a year. He is always here with and within me. How wonderful it was to know that I do not have to wait for a certain day to come, but I can relate to my Father anytime and always.

Can you see and feel this, child of God?

The memories that are very clear of my life are those of my mom raising us as a single parent most of the time. When my dad came home in the fortnight, he would arrive on a Friday evening, some days he would find me in bed already so I would see him in the morning on the Saturday.

No need to impress, kind of Father

I grew up a Jehovah's Witness, so we had books that we read. One specific book for kids is titled, My book of Bible stories. My dad would give me a chapter to read on Saturday morning and say when he returns in the evening I must tell him what I have read and its relevance to our lives. So I would spend my Saturday afternoon making sure that when he returned in the evening I have read everything and would tell him what I had learned from the book.

I always felt that I needed to impress him as my dad, so he would be proud of me. I don't know why I felt that way, but that is how I felt and would give it my all really, to understand what I was reading and its relevance to our lives.

Looking back I am grateful for that life skill I learned during those times, it is still relevant to my life in that whenever I look at something I should look at it analytically. That is how it went every time my dad visited. So I needed to make sure that when he returned I explained to him and depending on my explanation I would either see acceptance or disappointment in his eyes. He never taught me how to even study the book and apply the principle of relevance to our lives; it was as if he expected that skill to be there naturally.

He grants me the desires of my heart

Is there anything that you like but that is not available for you always? I am a meat lover, I usually joke and say that when my mom was weaning me from breastmilk she probably gave me meat because the way I love meat, it is just something else. My mom knew that and everyone in my family knew that Nomsa just loves meat and she must always have a big piece of meat in her plate and they all nurtured my love for meat. Now you see, my dad just did not understand that. How can a Girl Child be given so much meat in her plate? So his visits were always accompanied by him blaming mama as to why she was dishing up so much meat for me and that made me not really look forward to his visits.

A part of me was looking forward to my dad coming home because I needed him in my life, but then when it came to eating time I really didn't like it.

In one way or another, my mom would be caught up between keeping the peace and giving a smaller portion of meat knowing that it hurts me or giving me my usual portion size at the risk of hearing my dad blaming her for the portion size given.

You can imagine if for about twelve days you have meat portions to your satisfaction and then for two days you either get small portions or you will get the usual portions at the risk of hearing how a girl should not be given so much meat in her plate. So, his visits always gave me mixed emotions, on both the meat portions I would get and the approval look or disapproval look if I didn't meet his standards in terms of the explanation of what I had read. I would be caught between my desire for my dad to be home and the feelings I would get when things didn't go the way he wanted them to.

Father defined by actions

These were defining moments in my life in terms of shaping my outlook of a father figure and how they treat you if you do not meet their standards. When my dad was not home, we had daily devotionals using Daily Text and there was never any pressure that I got from my mom, it was fun and it was easy going. The tension always came when my dad came home because he had standards that were never placed on me by my mom.

I learned that when it comes to your relationship with your dad, you cannot afford to make a mistake, you must always be in order, and show just how much you know and understand things. When it comes to my love for meat and my dad always saying that they should never dish up so much meat for me as a girl, my mom is spoiling me, what was being engraved in me is that you should never be given what you really love to your satisfaction because that is spoiling you. It made an impression in me that there are certain things that must be given in limits not according to your desires.

So growing up, even though I desired certain things deep down I didn't believe that I deserve them as there would be times when I felt that I was falling short of what God expected from me as His child as a result I don't even deserve to get what I am desiring. I remember there were times when I would be applying for jobs, I would be called to interviews and if I don't get the position I would check if during that time I was faithful in my tithes. If it happened that in that month things were tight and I was not faithful I would feel God was justified in not giving me the position. After all I was not faithful in obeying His word so why should He give me what I desire.

I found that tithing for me was out of duty, the need to impress Him and always be in His good books rather than obedience out of love and knowing that as a Princess in the family. I bring my tithes because I love my Daddy not because I need to stay in His good books. I was kind of messed up in my mind in a big way you see, but thank God for bringing me to order in His love.

This is the interpretation that my little mind, growing up made and it determined how I related to people who hold the position of a father figure in my life. I became a pleaser to such people because I needed their approval so much, their approval meant a lot to me.

Meeting the Lord Jesus Christ

As I grew up, one day I met the Lord Jesus and accepted Him as Lord and Savior of my life. That was a defining moment in my life which I will always cherish for it opened up a new world that I am still enjoying even to this day. I was told that God is a Father who loves me, my mind and everything on the inside of me found that very hard to believe or accept. The word of God in Isaiah 49:16 which says I have engraved you in the palm of my hands, your walls are continually before me, it left me with a bitter taste somehow.

I could not believe that I am truly engraved in the palm of His hands. I would read or hear that I am the apple of His eye, having studied biology and knowing the apple of the eye, and that it is integral part of who you are, and I just found that hard to take and comprehend. I knew that and I would say it with my mouth but somehow deep down there was a battle within me, as I always felt and believed, that to be truly that I needed to do something.

In that area of my life I was an unbelieving believer, because as much as I believed, I didn't truly believe it. For me it was more about having to work in order to earn the love of God, the message of grace was hard to take in. I always felt the need to prove to God just how much I know and in relying in my own effort to prove to Him I mostly came short of His standard. So it was a constant internal struggle within me, and I could not share it with anyone.

There were lies that I believed for a long time about my heavenly Father and how I should relate to Him. I believed that I needed to impress Him, I thought He does not want to give me what I love, even though He can. I can never have the best of it all because that is spoiling. I would read the word and find that within me there was a battle going on because what I read and what I believe just did not relate.

The word says *"Delight yourself also in the Lord, and He shall give you the desires of your heart"* Psalm 37:4. To me the interpretation to delight in Him meant that I must do all I can to impress Him even if it meant faking it. I never knew what it really meant to delight in the Lord and with each desire not met, it confirmed what I believed in deep down and that gave the devil even more power over me.

Taking my position as Princess

I thank God for never giving up on me, for loving me and continuously drawing me to Himself. One day I attended a women's conference, and the Lord had an appointment with me, through His servant He called me to tell me just how much He loves me. He spoke through His servant that He loves me and said to me every time I pray I must see myself sitting on His lap, and He told her to give me a hug. If you have never been hugged by God ask me I know how it feels, it was not the lady who was hugging me, but God Himself and boy it felt so good, I melted and wept so much and I felt the Lord wiping those tears.

Now, this was in 2010, you can imagine the shock to my system when the Lord said to me I need to see myself sitting in His lap, I have never sat in my dad's lap, I don't know how to do it, I don't even know how it feels, but this

Dear Girl Child

is the level my Daddy was calling me to. There was joy on the inside of me and there was disbelief.

How can it be that my Father tells me this, is He not the kind of Dad that I need to impress? Is He not the one who truly does not want to give me the best of what I need; now He is calling me to His lap?

I had seen my husband put our boys in his lap and I know deep down that when they were young they truly loved that. There was a part of me that envied that and wondered what it feels like, and here at this moment in church the Lord said I want you to see yourself in my lap and He hugged me.

Precious daughter of God let me tell you, if you have never experienced the love of the Father you have not started enjoying life as a believer. Before I came to truly comprehend the love that my Daddy has for me as His princess, I was a mess inside. Outside it all seemed well but I knew it, Daddy knew that there were things that needed to be made right and He was the only one who could make it right.

You see, there is love that can only be given or showered by our Daddy to His princess, that there is no human being that can shower such kind of love. It is therefore important precious daughter, to allow Him to shower you with this love. It is not a mistake that you picked up this book, whether you bought it yourself or it was given to you as a gift, Daddy wants to love you through it.

If you are like me, and have not experienced the full love of your natural dad, sometimes it is not because they did not really love us, but they loved us in their own way, therefore allow Daddy to love you.

I learnt the hard way and at times placed demands on my husband because I needed him to fill the space that can only be filled by my Daddy.

He is my husband and has the responsibility to love me as a husband and he does that and I am grateful to God for his love, but when you have a void that needs to be filled with God, you place so much pressure on another human being which is unfair and it is not good for both of you as well as your marriage.

Daddy told me in 2010 that I should see myself sitting in His lap so I needed to learn to sit in His lap, you can imagine the battle within, as the enemy also comes and whispers negativity. It's been five years now and I must say that it keeps getting engraved inside of me. I believe that I am His princess, I can see myself on His lap and it feels soooooooo good.

God has a sense of humor I always say that. Sometimes I know that when I am praying I am sitting in His lap and some days when I am faced with serious life challenges I tend to forget that and it is in the midst of those times that my Daddy says to me, Princess do you remember that you are mine, do you remember that right now in the midst of your pain, the questions that you are asking sitting in my lap, I am attentive to every emotion that you are going through. When He does that, it feels like a light bulb has been switched ON and I sober up no matter how swallowed up, I was by my situation.

So precious daughter you are loved by God, you are special to Him and there is nothing He wants more than to shower you with love and for you to believe that you are His princess who is loved. There is no greater love than His love for you, believe that, let it sink in and no matter what you may face in life never ever treat yourself lower than the princes you are. You are royalty, live like royalty as the Lord ushers you in a place only He can usher you to.

14

CONFESSIONS

The Word of God in Job 22:28 says "You will also declare a thing, and it will be established for you; so light will shine on your ways." Therefore Girl Child, confess these words:

I am a child of God, the daughter of the Most High God;
I am the beloved of the Lord, highly favored by my Father;
I am made in the image of God, I look like God, walk like God, and have my being in God;
I am born of God, I am who My Father says I am;
I am the workmanship of God, being perfected every single day;
My Father in heaven loves me unconditionally, His love is immeasurable;
I live by the grace of God;
I appreciate myself for I am wonderfully and fearfully made;
I am one of a kind on this earth, there I no one who is like me;
I have been born for a great purpose on this earth;
I can do all things through Christ who strengthens me;
I am useful and I assist others who are in need;
I take care of my body;
I appreciate other girls around me;
I do not put down other girls, I lift them up so I have company at the top;

Dear Girl Child

I am destined for greatness;
I appreciate my journey, for it is a great journey;
I will achieve in life, for I am more than a conqueror in
Christ Jesus;
The world awaits for the great work that I will do for the
glory of God my Father;
I appreciate other people but I fear God;
I sit in the company of great God fearing and God loving
women;
I appreciate the wisdom of girls who have come before
me;
I also support other girls that are coming after me;
I am making a mark in history, my name shall be recorded
in history;
I am not put down by circumstances and disappoint-
ments, I am stronger than my enemies;
I forgive those that have hurt me, I let it to God, for my
sins have been forgiven, so I forgive;
I have been redeemed, bought at the price, the precious
blood of Jesus;
I put away all anger and bitterness, I put on grace upon
grace;
I live my life free of hurt and anger;
I am born for such a time such as this, to make my mark in
history;
I am a giver, it shall be given to me, pressed down, run-
ning over;
I believe the word of God concerning my life;
I am living and walking towards the vision of God for my
life;
I walk by faith, I believe in the things unseen, the things
unspoken of, the things revealed by God;

I will do greater works than the works done by Jesus;

I am not enticed by the riches of men, my sufficiency is from the Lord;

My God teaches me how to make wealth;

The riches hidden in dark places are brought to me by my Father;

I get things from God, I go down on my knees before my Father in heaven;

The rejection of men does not shape me, for I am accepted by the Lord in the beloved;

I do not give to be recognized by men, to get validation from men, but I give and look towards God;

My reward is with my Father;

The Lord has deposited strength within me, I have the ability to succeed;

I shall be counted amongst the great women of God from now forward;

I am dear to the heart of God, a royal diadem in the palm of the hand of God, the apple of God's eye;

I am a daughter of the Most High God.

About the author

Dear Girl Child is the third published book by **Carol Nkambule.** She has moved from being an author to being a publisher. This is the fourth book published by her company Kingdom Anchored, the first to be authored and published by her.

Her first two titles, *From the Pit to the Palace* and *Victorious Youth* exposed the author in her. It is her ambition to elevate the written word, the gospel, through books.

Academically, she has an MBA and B.com Honours. With her family behind her, she surely is arising to make a mark in the history of her generation.

Called into the Apostolic Office, she is still at Bible College and ministers at the local church.

May the girls enjoy this inspirational letter from the heart of God.

Contact the author through:

Email: carolnkambule@gmail.com

Website: www.kingdomanchored.co.za

www.wordxplosion.co.za